Praises for
Top 10 Reasons Some People Go to Hell...
and the One Reason No One Ever Has to!

"Of all of the doctrines revealed in the Bible, from humanity's perspective, soteriology, or the doctrine of salvation, would certainly be the most important since a correct understanding and response to this doctrine determines where a soul spends eternity: heaven or hell. Yet, despite its importance, the evangelical church seems to be growing progressively inaccurate and even apathetic concerning how the great salvation truths of Scripture are communicated to the lost. It is possible to miss out on a joyful eternity with God simply by misunderstanding or misconstruing the simplicity of the gospel. That is why I am delighted with this new volume written by my friend Dr. J. B. Hixson, which not only argues for the simplicity of the gospel but also holds forth its truth in light of perpetual misunderstandings of it. I am always delighted to endorse Dr. Hixson's work as he is one of the few scholars who correctly understands the true grace position of Scripture and also holds to dispensational premillennialism. Consequently, he has the right theology necessary to rightly divide the Word of God on this critically important topic."

- *Dr. Andy Woods, pastor-teacher, Sugar Land Bible Church, TX; President, Chafer Theological Seminary, NM*

"Many theologians have a tendency to muddy the waters of the gospel. In contrast, Dr. Hixson's book, *Top 10 Reasons*, clears away the confusion and focuses on the straightforward message of God's good news. For those who know the Lord, this book is a fresh reminder of what it means to simply believe in Christ for salvation. It is also an excellent resource for pointing the unbelieving skeptic, as well as the confused Christian, to the clear message of the gospel."

Bob Nyberg, retired missionary, Ethnos360, FL

"The Apostle Paul was concerned about the Corinthians when he wrote these words: "But I fear, lest somehow, as the serpent deceived Eve by his craftiness, so your minds may be corrupted from the simplicity that is in Christ" (2 Corinthians 11:3, NKJV). The gospel of eternal life by grace alone through faith alone in Christ alone is a simple gospel. In a day of murky presentations of the gospel of Christ, Hixson ... reminds us all not to complicate the good news. This work will function well as an extended gospel tract that can be given to unbelievers to help them come to trust in Christ for salvation. It will also help believers to understand some of the pitfalls they will face as they share their faith. Make this book one that you will read this year."

Dr. Mike Stallard, Director of International Ministry, Friends of Israel Gospel Ministry, NJ

"As Jesus prophesied when asked about the end of the age, we are today experiencing the greatest deception the world has ever seen. The need for a work like *Top 10 Reasons* cannot be overestimated. Like the truth that it exposes, it is clear, concise, easy to read, simple, and magnificently freeing to the soul. It can become a great soul-winning tool as believers distribute it into the hands of the lost. Greater still, it can help pastors and preachers remain true to the simple gospel to which we were called in an age when so many are falling prey to the subtle temptations of Satan and the flesh to add to, and thus destroy, the perfect gospel of Jesus Christ."

Dr. Wayne Dartez, Victory Baptist Church, Lake Charles, LA

"Everyone should read *Top 10 Reasons Some People Go to Hell* by Dr. J. B. Hixson. In a world where politeness and social convention often keep us from speaking the truth, Dr. Hixson boldly proclaims the message of the Bible. If there is one book for a non-Christian to read on Christianity, let it be this one. Everyone needs to understand the eternal reality that is at stake. Powerful illustrations, approachable language, and Hixson's inimitable writing style will leave even the most antagonistic reader with a robust understanding of the Good News of salvation. For a believer, this book will sharpen your clarity and understanding of the gospel message. It will motivate and prepare you to share it with everyone you can before it is too late. Helpful discussion questions make this an excellent resource for any church, sermon series, workshop, or Bible study group of any kind. Whether your goal is to understand your faith better, grow spiritually, be better equipped to do the work of an evangelist, or simply have a great resource that you can share with anybody, this book is for you."

Brad Maston, author and pastor-teacher, Fort Collins Bible Church, Fort Collins, CO

"J. B. Hixson brings clarity to the most important issue there is: how to have eternal life. *Top 10 Reasons Some People Go to Hell* carefully explains how the gospel is a good-news message about forgiveness of sins through one moment of faith in Jesus alone. Hixson refutes the Pharisaic approach to salvation which, sadly, runs amok in the evangelical world. He also dismantles obstacles preventing many from considering God's free offer of eternal life. Hixson gently presents God's simple plan of salvation to any reader seeking the truth. Readers will be plainly shown how the Bible teaches that if anyone goes to Hell, it is because he or she "has not believed in the name of the only begotten Son of God" (John 3:18).

Adam Lair, professor, Cornerstone Bible Institute, SD

"I cannot overstate the impact that Dr. Hixson's writing has had on me personally. Even though I am not a Bible college graduate, I have had the blessing and privilege of receiving a Bible college education in the pew under several gifted Bible teachers, among whom J. B. Hixson is chief. From the time that I first heard him speak on the radio and sat under his teaching, I have been blessed by his careful, clear, and consistent focus on the Bible as our sole authority for all beliefs, attitudes, and practices. I have read all of his works, distributed them to friends and family, and rely on them in the prison ministry where I currently serve. His focus on the clear and accurate Gospel has been especially encouraging to me. His latest work is no different. Have your Bible close and get ready to feed to the fullest. May the Lord bless you as you seek to know Him deeper through the reading and study of this important and relevant topic."

Jim Cochran, Bible study leader, Prison Ministry

This is a rare book and one that needed to be written. I'm glad that Dr. Hixson is the one who wrote it because this isn't really a book: It's a friend-to-friend conversation a master author is having with you, the reader. From the get-go, you realize that Dr. Hixson cares — really cares — about the gospel and your need to hear and believe it. He imprints every page with an urgency little heard today from pulpit or page. Dr. Hixson soaks every pertinent point with Scripture while packing each paragraph with provocative thought as each word marches toward a biblical conclusion. This is one of those books to have and to hold, to treasure, to savor, then to share with others.

Dr. Michael Halsey, Chancellor, Grace Biblical Seminary

TOP 10 REASONS

SOME PEOPLE GO TO

HELL

AND THE

ONE REASON

NO ONE EVER HAS TO!

TOP 10 REASONS
SOME PEOPLE GO TO
HELL
AND THE
ONE REASON
NO ONE EVER HAS TO!

J. B. Hixson

LARKSPUR, COLORADO

Grace Acres Press
PO Box 22
Larkspur, CO 80118
www.GraceAcresPress.com

Grace Acres Press also publishes books in a variety of electronic formats. Some content that appears in print may not be available in electronic books.

All Scripture quotations taken from the *New King James Version* unless otherwise indicated.
ESV: *English Standard Version*
KJV: *King James Version*
NASB: *New American Standard Bible*
NIV: *New International Version*
NLT: *New Living Translation*

Some portions of this book have been adapted from the author's previously published works, including articles, blogs, sermons, and books.

Print ISBN: 978-1-60265-072-5
E-book ISBN: 978-1-60265-073-2
Library of Congress Control Number: 2020937600

Printed in United States of America
25 24 23 22 21 20   01 02 03 04 05 06 07 08

Dedication

To Lynn and Tami Rutland and all of my dear friends at
the San Juan Mountain Church

*"A friend is always loyal, and a brother is born
to help in time of need."* (Proverbs 17:17, NLT)

Acknowledgments

I wish to thank the following people:

- My wife, Wendy, without whom my life and ministry would mean nothing (Proverbs 18:22).

- My children, who bring me joy and pride beyond measure.

- The many supporters of Not By Works Ministries, without whom this book would not have been possible.

- North Routt Community Church, for unconditionally loving my family.

- My mom and dad, for always being there for me and my family.

- My publisher, Anne Fenske, and Grace Acres Press.

- Jeff Holt, for his friendship, support, and invaluable help in editing this manuscript.

- Cindy Wallen, for her gracious and faithful help with Not By Works Ministries.

- My friends and colleagues at Cornerstone Bible Institute, in Hot Springs, South Dakota.

- Dr. Bruce Waltke, for his excellent insights on Psalm 90, many of which found their way into chapter 11 of this book.

- Dr. Tom Constable, my friend and former professor, for his amazing expository notes which influenced much of the biblical commentary in this book.

- Lynn and Tami Rutland and our friends at San Juan Mountain Church, to whom this book is dedicated.

I need no other argument,
I need no other plea;
It is enough that Jesus died,
And that He died for me.

My faith has found a resting place,
Not in device nor creed;
I trust the Ever-living One,
His wounds for me shall plead.

Enough for me that Jesus saves,
This ends my fear and doubt;
A sinful soul I come to Him,
He'll never cast me out.

My heart is leaning on the Word,
The written Word of God,
Salvation by my Savior's name,
Salvation through His blood.

My great Physician heals the sick,
The lost He came to save;
For me His precious blood He shed,
For me His life He gave.

I need no other argument,
I need no other plea;
It is enough that Jesus died,
And that He died for me.

—Eliza Edmunds Hewitt (1891)

Table of Contents

Preface

It is likely that the premise of this book will not sit well with some people, due to its controversial subject matter and provocative title, *Top 10 Reasons Some People Go to Hell*. I anticipate reactions that run the gamut from intrigue to incredulity to indignation. Some might even identify what they see as a palpable attitude of arrogance and presumption on my part. After all, who do I think I am to suggest that some people will go to hell? And on top of that, how dare I claim to know why they go there?!

Before you set this book aside, however, or hastily conclude that it is just another example of misguided ramblings from an overzealous theologian, let me ask you to at least finish reading this preface. Give me a chance to make the case that this is a worthwhile topic by outlining some of my foundational presuppositions. If you disagree with these presuppositions after reading the preface, you are under no obligation to continue reading. (Of course, you are under no obligation to read the preface, either, but now that you have started, I hope you will keep reading.)

Underlying the title, *Top 10 Reasons Some People Go to Hell*, are some implicit assumptions: *There is a hell. There is a heaven. Not everyone goes to heaven. Some people go to hell.* You may agree with these assumptions or you may disagree with them. Regardless, it is important to understand that these assumptions flow from certain presuppositions: timeless axioms such as "Absolute truth exists," and "There is an ultimate standard for right and wrong." If these axioms are correct—and I believe they are—then the matter comes down to this question: *What is the ultimate standard?* That is a great question, for our assumptions are only as good as our presuppositions, and our presuppositions are only as reliable as the standard upon which they are based.

I will admit that there is widespread disagreement over the accuracy of my presuppositions. Many people reject the notions that *absolute truth exists and there is an ultimate standard for right and wrong.* We must remember, however, that disagreement proves neither inaccuracy nor uncertainty. In other words, the fact that some people disagree with these presuppositions is not evidence that these presuppositions are wrong, nor is it evidence that they are unclear. For example, the number of people who disagree with the assertion that $2 + 2 = 4$ has no bearing on the accuracy or clarity of the equation. All assertions must stand or fall on their own merit. There is no such thing as truth by consensus. Truth, unlike beauty, is not in the eye of the beholder.

The premise of this book is based upon fundamental presuppositions that are not the result of internal philosophical musings, personal opinions, or speculative conjecture. Rather, they flow from an external standard that I believe serves as the only basis for our beliefs, attitudes, and practices: *the Bible*. It is my contention that the Bible serves as the filter for any and all truth claims. You may disagree, but if you will grant me a little latitude as I lay out the case, I think you will find that the Bible has proven itself to be trustworthy and reliable again and again. At the very least, it deserves a seat at the table in the discussion of the ultimate standard for truth.

The Bible claims within its own pages to be the Word of God—the Creator of the universe. More than 3,800 times the Bible declares, "Thus says the Lord." The Bible also states that "every Word of God is *pure*" (Proverbs 30:5). The psalmist reminds us "therefore all Your precepts concerning all things I consider to be *right*"

(Psalm 119:128). Again, in Psalm 119:75, we read, "I know, O LORD, that Your judgments are right." According to the Bible, "the law of the Lord is perfect" (Psalm 19:7), and "the judgments of the LORD are true" (Psalm 19:9).

It is significant that the Bible describes itself as "pure," "right," "perfect," and "true." From the outset, readers of the Bible are forced to grapple with this self-proclamation. Is the Bible really *true ... right ... even perfect*? Or is it a book written by a delusional author making empty, boastful claims? There really is no middle ground. Either the Bible is what it claims to be, or it is entirely unreliable on its face. It is my belief that the Bible is trustworthy. Allow me to explain why I believe this.

I trust the Bible because it is in a class by itself when compared with all other books. It was written over a period of 1,500 years, by some forty different human authors, in three different languages, spanning three continents. Yet its continuity and consistency are nothing short of astonishing — miraculous, really. The only plausible explanation is divine authorship. There must be a supernatural thread tying the whole of Scripture together. The Bible is God's way of saying, "Here I am. Look at Me." A perfect Creator demands a perfect representation in His Word. In the Bible, the Creator of the universe has given us "everything we need for life and godliness" (2 Peter 1:3). It is a "lamp to our feet and a light to our path" (Psalm 119:105). The Bible is more than a rulebook: it is a roadmap.

I trust the Bible because as a roadmap it shows a broken world how to be reconciled to its Creator. The Bible's message goes from creation to corruption to redemption. It is a beauty to ashes back to beauty story. As the narrative of human history unfolds in the Bible, we learn how God makes beautiful things from broken things; we see how He graciously steps in to fix a problem that we created by our own free will; we learn how He paid a debt

He did not owe; we witness His unconditional love as He makes all things new once again. The roadmap of the Bible takes us on a journey to peace and reconciliation that cannot be found any other way. Like a treasure map with just one "X," the Bible provides the *only* solution to humankind's sin problem.

I trust the Bible because, as the Word of God, it is "alive and active" (Hebrews 4:12). Like a double-edged sword, it pierces through all of the deception, confusion, and uncertainty that the world's philosophy brings and cuts right to the heart of the matter. As Howard Hendricks once remarked, "When you read any other book on the planet, you are doing something to it, but when you read the Bible, it is doing something to you." It is a "discerner of our thoughts" (Hebrews 4:12), a searcher of our souls. It offers hope to a desperate world where men, women, and children are crying out for help.

I trust the Bible because its message is unique. Unlike every other religion or man-made solution, the hope that the Bible offers is *free*. It comes at no cost to the recipient. That is what sets the message of God's Word apart. It proclaims good news that brings great joy, not bad information that brings greater burdens. This good news is what the Bible calls the Gospel. The Gospel message is simple and profound: At a time when humankind was hopeless and helpless, God sent His eternal Son, Jesus Christ, to the earth to pay humanity's penalty for sin. In the pages that follow, I am going to unpack the Gospel message in greater detail. I will explain that there are many reasons some people may end up in hell, but there is one important reason—and only one—that no one ever has to.

I trust the Bible because the truth of God's Word is steadfast and resolute. It withstands the revolution of change. The psalmist declared, "*Forever*, O LORD, Your word is settled in heaven" (Psalm 119:89). He writes, "the righteousness of Your testimonies is *everlasting*" (Psalm 119:144), and again, "Concerning Your testimonies, I have known of old that You have founded them *forever*" (Psalm 119:152). At a time when truth has become a social construct, formulated from prejudices and ever-shifting opinions rather than timeless absolutes, the principles of God's Word provide an anchor in the storm—a true north on the roadmap of life.

Not only does the Bible withstand the revolution of change, but it also endures the ravages of time. "Every one of Your righteous judgments *endures forever*" (Psalm 119:160). I trust the Bible because the archaeological evidence testifies to the divine nature of this book. Although the New Testament was written in the first century AD, today, nearly two thousand years later, we have thousands upon thousands of manuscript fragments dating from as early as the second century AD. No book on the planet has ever been preserved to this scope and magnitude. Let me give you some examples.

Tacitus was a first-century Roman historian. Much of our ancient history today, as detailed in academic history books, is based upon his writings, yet we have only two surviving manuscripts of his works. Thucydides was an influential Athenian historian who lived and wrote in the fifth century BC. We have only eight surviving manuscripts of his works. Herodotus, another Greek historian, was a contemporary of Thucydides. Only eight of his manuscripts have survived the ravages of time. Euripides, a Greek playwright, also lived and wrote in the fifth century BC. We have only nine of his ancient manuscripts today. Nevertheless, scholars depend on these writings for information about the world these authors lived in and wrote about.

In contrast, we have *more than six thousand* ancient manuscripts of the New Testament available today! By comparison to the preserved writings of these other influential historical figures from the same era, this is nothing short of astonishing. No one questions the veracity and trustworthiness of ancient historians such as Herodotus or Thucydides, whose works are far less historically verifiable than the Word of God. Why do so many doubt the Bible's trustworthiness? I trust the Bible because of the miraculous way in which it has been preserved through the centuries. Almost all of the human authors of Scripture gave their lives because they believed in its message. Many of the early church fathers who helped preserve the manuscripts of the Bible likewise paid the ultimate price. From the beginning, people knew there was something unique about this book.

Finally, I trust the Bible because, simply put, it works. Time and again I have seen the value of the Word of God in my personal life. When I do not know which way to turn, it points me in the right direction. When I am down and discouraged, it lifts me up. When I am confused, it clarifies. When I am hurting, it heals. When I am weak, it strengthens. The Bible has been a continual source of reassurance for me. It tells me more about my Creator, and the more I learn about Him, the more I trust Him. Like the psalmist some three thousand years ago, I have found "wonderful things" in the Bible (Psalm 119:18).

What about you? Do you trust the Bible as the only standard for your beliefs, attitudes, and practices? If you grant the premise that "the entirety of God's word is truth," and "every one of His righteous judgments *endures forever*" (Psalm 119:160), then the assumptions upon which *Top 10 Reasons Some People Go to Hell* are based are undeniable: *There is a hell. There is a heaven. Not everyone goes to heaven. Some people go to hell.* These assumptions will be understood and accepted readily by those who believe in a literal interpretation of the Bible. Indeed, only the most fanciful treatment of Scripture could lead someone to reject the realities of a literal heaven and a literal hell.

Nevertheless, I realize that some of you do not accept the authority of God's Word as the only filter for truth claims. Still others value the Bible, but do not accept its plain teaching from a literal, grammatical, historical framework. Therefore, for many of you the source of truth remains an open question. To you I say: *that is okay*. The search for truth is crucial and cannot, and should not, be rushed. All I can ask is that you consider the arguments set forth in the following pages. Do not accept my conclusions merely because I declare them. At the same time, however, do not reject my conclusions without giving them due consideration. Read this book with a critical eye, for "condemnation without investigation is the height of ignorance," as Albert Einstein reminded us. So, investigate. Study. Consider. If I am wrong, you have only lost a few hours of time, and hopefully you learned a few things of some redeeming value along the way.

Suppose I am right, however. The matters discussed in *Top 10 Reasons Some People Go to Hell* are not insignificant or trivial. This book addresses matters of eternal consequence. That alone should motivate you to keep investigating before condemning. If I am right, and the Bible is to be trusted, that means there is a literal place of eternal torment called hell, and *no one has to go there*. Even if, in your mind, there is only a remote possibility that hell exists, doesn't it makes sense to investigate how to avoid it, just in case? What if one of the common reasons people end up in hell applies to you? Wouldn't you want someone to sound the warning? The reality of eternal torment has been addressed by thousands of religions and faith traditions for many millennia. Clearly it is a subject that should not be summarily dismissed. Why not let the Bible weigh in?

Moreover, if I am right, and the Bible is to be trusted, that means there also is a literal place of eternal bliss called heaven, and *anyone can go there*. Doesn't it makes sense to investigate how you can be rescued from hell and spend eternity in heaven? The pursuit of heaven has occupied an enormous place in the minds of millions, if not billions, of people throughout human history. Do you really want to dismiss the notion of heaven out of hand without examining the evidence? Why not see what the Bible has to say about it?

Many of you who do accept my presupposition that the Bible is the filter for all truth claims have already come to understand and believe the Gospel message that it proclaims. You accept that the only way to avoid the eternal penalty of sin is to place your faith in Jesus Christ, the Son of God, who died and rose again for your sins. You have embraced the truth that Jesus is the only One who can save you. If that is the case, my prayer for you is that this book will equip you in helping others to understand and believe the Gospel. By presenting and explaining some of the reasons people reject the Gospel, this book can be a helpful aid to your evangelistic endeavors.

Others of you, whether you accept my premise that the Bible is trustworthy or not, may still be working through the message of God's Word regarding salvation. Perhaps you have not yet come to the point of trusting in Jesus Christ, and Him alone, as your only hope of salvation. For you, I hope and pray that this book serves to bring you to a point where you choose to believe the words of Jesus when He said, "Most assuredly, I say to you, he who believes in Me has everlasting life" (John 6:47). As you read the pages that follow, and interact with the biblical arguments I make, I pray that you will be convicted of "sin, righteousness, and judgment" (John 16:8) and place your faith in the One who paid your penalty and offers to you the forgiveness of sins and the free gift of eternal life.

J. B. H.

1

The Bomb and the Explosion

He who believes in Him is not condemned; but he who
does not believe is condemned already, because he has not
believed in the name of the only begotten Son of God.
—Jesus Christ (John 3:18)

Why do some people go to hell when they die? That is the question at hand. At its core, this is a theological question, and the Bible speaks directly to it. Theologically, there is only one reason anyone ends up in hell: *unbelief.* When someone dies having never believed the Gospel, that person will spend eternity in a literal place of torment called hell. Jesus put it this way, "He who believes in [Me] is not condemned; but he who does not believe is condemned already, because he has not believed in the name of the only begotten Son of God" (John 3:18). He added, "Most assuredly, I say to you, he who hears My word and believes in Him who sent Me has everlasting life, and shall not come into judgment, but has passed from death into life" (John 5:24).

In other words, the only way to avoid condemnation and eternal judgment is to believe in Jesus Christ, the Son of God, who died and rose again for your sins. "If you do not believe that I am He, you will die in your sins," Jesus said (John 8:24), and to die in your sins means to face eternal torment (Matthew 25:41; Luke 12:4–5, 16:23; Revelation 20:10–14). According to Jesus, "He who believes in the Son has everlasting life; and he who does not believe in the Son shall not see life, but the wrath of God abides on him" (John 3:36). More than 160 times in the New Testament, eternal life is conditioned solely upon faith in Jesus

Christ. Jesus said plainly, "Most assuredly, I say to you, he who believes in Me has everlasting life" (John 6:47). Believing the Gospel — the good news that Jesus Christ died for your sins and rose from the dead — is the only way to avoid the penalty of sin: namely, hell.

Although the theology is unambiguous, the question "Why do some people go to hell when they die?" is not merely theological; it is also practical. There is a secondary aspect to this question that is equally relevant. Namely, *why* do people fail to believe the Gospel? Disbelief leads to hell; but what leads to disbelief? What life experiences or thought processes might influence someone to reject the free gift of eternal life? Faith, by definition, is inherently an intellectual exercise. You cannot believe something you do not comprehend.

The biblical word for faith, *pistis*, means "confidence or assurance in a stated proposition." To believe something means you are confident that it is true. To disbelieve something means you do not think it is true. Contrary to the assertions of some, faith is not an emotional response. It is an intellectual response. It takes place in the mind. That is why Paul describes unbelievers as those "whose *minds* the god of this age has blinded, who *do not believe*, lest the light of the gospel ... shine on them" (2 Corinthians 4:4).

Asking "Why do some people go to hell?" is really two questions in one. It is like asking, "Why did Abraham Lincoln die? Was it because of a gunshot wound to the head, or because his heart stopped beating?" The answer is: *both*. Ultimately, Abraham Lincoln died because his heart stopped beating, but his heart stopped beating because he was shot in the head. Why do some people end up in hell? Because they never believed the Gospel. Why didn't they believe the Gospel? That is the question this book seeks to answer.

To use another analogy: Which is more destructive, a *bomb* or the *explosion* that comes from the bomb? It is hard to separate the two; one stems directly from the other. Similarly, when it comes to hell, there is a bomb and there is an explosion. The explosion (unbelief) is the ultimate reason anyone ends up in hell. The person never believed the Gospel. Yet, the deafening explosion of unbelief can result from a variety of bombs: various influences and thinking errors. In the following chapters, we will look at some of the most common reasons people refuse to believe the Gospel. First, however, let us examine the theological elements of this question a little further.

Sin and Death

When God created humankind, He made us in His image, according to His divine design. "So God created man in His own image; in the image of God He created him; male and female He created them" (Genesis 1:27). Part of this "image of God" in man includes volition, or *free will*. God did not create a class of robots, who, like puppets on a string, are forced to do only what their master demands. He created us as free moral beings. Because of His deep love for us, He warned us from the outset about the danger of not obeying His instructions. He cautioned us to avoid the one tree in the Garden whose fruit was poisonous. "All who eat from it will die," He said (Genesis 2:16 17). Despite God's warning, we chose to disobey. We ignored God's admonition and reaped the consequences. This initial choice we made is what the Bible calls *sin*.

The human condition of sin is universal. "For all have sinned and fall short of the glory of God" (Romans 3:23). "There is not a righteous man on earth who does what is right and never sins" (Ecclesiastes 7:20, NIV). The result of sin is spiritual death; that is, we are separated from God and in need of reconciliation. "The wages of sin is death" (Romans 6:23). We are "born dead in our trespasses and sin" (Ephesians 2:1). We do not become sinners when we sin; we sin because we are sinners, and that is what sinners do. King David said, "Behold, I was brought forth in iniquity, and in sin my mother conceived me" (Psalm 51:5). Our very nature is corrupt and in need of redemption.

The objective, empirical source of the Bible is not the only way we know that sin is a universal problem. Our own personal experience also attests to this reality. Our own honest evaluation of the human condition must result in the conclusion that man is naturally predisposed to willful, unprovoked action that is disrespectful, damaging, and destructive. Throughout history, every culture known to man has had some concept of unacceptable behavior that is considered "bad" because it brings harm rather than good. The Bible speaks of this common knowledge about right and wrong when it says that even unbelievers have a "conscience [that] bears witness ... accusing or else excusing them" (Romans 2:15). "Woven into the very fabric of our creation," as Eugene Peterson put it, "is something deep within us that echoes God's yes and no, right and wrong." Lance Morrow, in a Time magazine article entitled "Evil," said, "Evil is a word we use when we come to the limit of human comprehension. But we sometimes suspect that it is the core of our true selves." He is right.

From the moment of conception, every human being is plagued with the disease of sin. "Therefore ... through one man sin entered the world, and death through sin, and thus death spread to *all men*, because all sinned" (Romans 5:12). Adam's sin in the Garden was passed down through the blood so that the entire human race is condemned. Left unremedied, we will "die in our sins," as Jesus said (John 8:24), and spend eternity in hell. This is the predicament we all find ourselves in apart from Christ. The good news is this: "God demonstrates His own love toward us, in that while we were still sinners, Christ died for us" (Romans 5:8).

The penalty for sin had to be paid. "Without the shedding of blood there is no forgiveness" (Hebrews 9:22, NASB). Jesus Christ took our sin upon Himself and purchased our redemption with His own blood. "In Him we have redemption through His blood, the forgiveness of sins, according to the riches of His grace" (Ephesians 1:7). When it comes to the sacrifice for sin, only a spotless lamb will do. We have been redeemed by "the precious blood of Christ, as of a lamb without blemish and without spot" (1 Peter 1:19). Jesus Christ, the eternal Son of God, left the realm of eternity and came to Earth where He lived a perfect, holy, sinless life and died a cruel death on the cross to pay for the sins of the whole world. "He Himself is the propitiation for our sins, and not for ours only but also for the whole world" (1 John 2:2). Through His only Son, God solved the problem of sin and death.

Faith Alone

How do we appropriate the payment for sin that Jesus made on our behalf? How is God's remedy given to us, exactly? Is it automatically applied to everyone? Or is there something we must do in order to receive it? As we mentioned earlier, more than 160 times the Bible conditions eternal life upon faith alone in Christ alone. The Bible is clear that *faith is the one and only way to avoid the penalty of sin and receive the gift of eternal life.* Salvation is a free gift. "The free gift of God is eternal life in Christ Jesus our Lord" (Romans 6:23, NASB). However, like all gifts, the gift of salvation must be received. A gift cannot be forced upon someone, and God will never force the free gift of eternal life upon us. We must receive it by faith. Forced love is not love at all; it is compulsion. As John Walvoord said, "No one is ever saved against his will."

> **A gift cannot be forced upon someone, and God will never force the free gift of eternal life upon us. We must receive it by faith.**

Eternal salvation can never be attained by our own efforts at moral improvement, through a promise or pledge to do better, through a commitment of some kind to God, through a willingness to stop sinning or improve our behavior, nor through any other effort that relegates eternal salvation to some type of two-way contract or agreement between God and man. When it comes to eternal salvation, Jesus paid it all. In the words of Augustus Toplady, "Nothing in my hands I bring; simply to Thy cross I cling!"

Salvation is not a bilateral contract in which we give something to God and in return He gives us eternal life. Rather, salvation is a unilateral gift. It is one-directional. There is one giver: *God*. There is one receiver: *man*. We receive the gift of eternal salvation, fully paid for by the blood of Christ, by trusting in Him and Him alone as the only one who can forgive our sin and save us from hell. When a lost sinner comes to God with his arms full of offerings that he hopes will satisfy the wrath of God against sin, he leaves no room for the grace of God. We must come empty-handed, with arms humbly open, our hands divested of any meager action, promise, pledge, or commitment that we think will impress a holy God. "To him who does not work but believes on Him who justifies the ungodly, his faith is accounted for righteousness" (Romans 4:5).

Two Births, One Death

When we believe the Gospel, in that very moment of belief, we are made alive. We pass from "death to life," as Jesus promised (John 5:24). Jesus told a Jewish leader named Nicodemus that the only way he could be saved from the penalty of sin is to be born from above. Jesus said, "Most assuredly, I say to you, unless one is born again, he cannot see the kingdom of God" (John 3:3). The phrase "born again" literally means "born from above." Nicodemus was confused by what Jesus said because he had never heard of the heavenly birth, the second birth. He only knew of the earthly birth, the physical birth. Jesus goes on to explain that entrance into heaven requires a second birth.

According to the Bible, if you are born only once (Ephesians 2:1), you will die twice (John 8:24; Revelation 20:14). However, if you are born twice (John 3:3), you will die only once (John 5:24). Let me explain. Every human being is born once, physically. Yet, as we have seen, we are born "dead in our trespasses and sin" (Ephesians 2:1). Though we are physically alive, we are

> **If you are born only once, you will die twice. If you are born twice, you will only die once.**

spiritually dead and separated from a holy God. Thus, we need a second birth, a new birth. If we never experience this new birth, we will not only die physically one day, but we also will experience what the Bible calls the "second death" (Revelation 20:14) and spend eternity in hell. If you are born only once, you will die twice. However, if you place your faith in Jesus Christ as the only One who can save you, and thereby experience the second birth, you will escape the second death. You will die physically someday, but the second death has no power over those who have been born from above. If you are born twice, you will only die once.

Physical death, for believers, is the golden key that unlocks the riches of eternity. "Precious in the sight of the Lord is the death of His saints" (Psalm 116:15). Once we have been made alive by faith in Christ (born again), "death is swallowed up in victory" (1 Corinthians 15:54). The Bible tells us, "For as in Adam all die, even so in Christ all shall be made alive" (1 Corinthians 15:22). Because the second death has no power over believers, when we die we go immediately to be in the presence of our Lord in heaven. "To be absent from the body [is] to be present with the Lord" (2 Corinthians 5:8).

Justice, Mercy, and Grace

When confronted with the notion of hell, many people immediately recoil. "How can a loving God allow anyone to go to hell?" they wonder. Such reasoning demonstrates a failure to understand the very nature of God as revealed in His self-revelation, the Bible. In particular, the suggestion that God should make sure that every human being escapes the horrors of hell evidences a lack of understanding about three key attributes of God: justice, mercy, and grace. Let's take a closer look at these three attributes.

Justice means *getting what you deserve.* It speaks to issues such as fairness, equity, dependability, and trustworthiness. If we go back to the Garden, and the creation of humankind, we recall that God made a declaration. He plainly stated that if we ignore His warning and eat the forbidden fruit we will die. Suppose, for the sake of argument, that after we ate the fruit, God had not followed through on His declaration. Suppose He reneged: humankind did not die and no one had to face hell. What would that tell us about God? It would mean that at best He is fickle, unfaithful, unreliable, and unjust. We could never count on anything He says because He violated His own Word.

I don't know about you, but for my part, I am glad that God is not fickle, that His Word can be trusted. I am glad that sin brought judgment just like God said it would. It means that God is just. We can sing the song of Moses, "Great and marvelous are Your works, Lord God Almighty! *Just and true are Your ways*, O King of the saints" (Revelation 15:3). The Apostle Paul declared that God is "just and the justifier of the one who has faith in Jesus" (Romans 3:26). God's intrinsic justice means that sin brings punishment, just as He said it would. That punishment was placed on the shoulders of God's Son and our Savior, Jesus Christ. Isaiah the prophet told us that when Christ came, He would "bring justice" to the world (Isaiah 42:1).

Mercy, in contrast, means *not getting punishment you deserve.* Mercy, like justice, is one of the eternal attributes of God. He is not more just than He is merciful, nor is He *more merciful* than He is just. He is equally just and merciful. Indeed, all of His eternal attributes are immutable. He cannot grow more merciful, nor can He become less just. As we just reviewed, His justice requires that sin be punished; similarly, His mercy requires that a solution be provided. God is "rich in mercy" (Ephesians 2:4), and it is "not by works of righteousness which we have done, but according to His mercy He saved us" (Titus 3:5).

Grace is different from both justice and mercy. Grace means *getting blessing you do not deserve.* Like mercy and justice, grace is one of God's eternal attributes, and it is no less important than any other attribute. Grace is a free gift of undeserved blessing. Eternal life is a gift of grace. We certainly do not deserve it. We are "justified freely by His grace through the redemption that is in Christ Jesus" (Romans 3:24). When we were dead in our trespasses and sins, deserving of hell, God "made us alive together with Christ — by grace you have been saved" (Ephesians 2:5). Our salvation is "according to the riches of His grace" (Ephesians 1:7). "For by grace you have been saved through faith, and that not of yourselves; it is the gift of God, not of works, lest anyone should boast" (Ephesians 2:8–9).

God's attributes are not independent of one another; they are *interdependent.* God described Himself to Moses as the eternal "I am" (Exodus 3:14). What He meant by this is, "There is not when I was not. And there shall not be when I cannot be." God is omnipotent, omniscient, and omnipresent. As one preacher put it, "There is no use in running from God, because when you take off running, God says, 'Good-bye;' and when you get to where you are going, God says, 'Hello!'" There never has been a time when God did not exist; there never will be a time when He does not exist; and all of His attributes never change. God is not subject to improvement, nor is He subject to deterioration. He can be trusted!

The difference between justice, mercy, and grace is important to understand. Consider the following illustration. Suppose a child disobeys his father and gets caught. As the youngster sits in front of his father, waiting to face the music, Dad says, "Did you break the rules?" The child responds, "Yes, Dad." Dad goes on, "You realize you deserve to be punished, right?" "Yes, Dad," replies the child, fearfully. At this point, if the father were to impose an appropriate punishment, that would be *justice*. The child would get what he deserved as a result of his own actions. If, on the other hand, the father was to withhold punishment from the child, saying merely, "Okay. Don't let it happen again," that would be mercy. However, if the father were to add, "Now, go grab your coat and let's go to Baskin Robbins for some ice cream," that would be *grace*.

Justice is getting what we deserve; *mercy* is not getting punishment we deserve; *grace* is getting undeserved blessing. Each of these three principles is present in relation to the issue of sin, hell, and salvation. At Calvary, God's justice, grace, and mercy all coalesce. Justice is served because Jesus died and paid the penalty for sin. Mercy is applied because eternal punishment in hell is withheld for those who believe the Gospel. Grace is given because those who believe the Gospel also receive the free,

> *Justice* is getting what we deserve; *mercy* is not getting punishment we deserve; *grace* is getting undeserved blessing.

undeserved gift of eternal life. We see all three of these elements in John 3:16: "For God so loved the world that He gave His only begotten Son [justice], that whoever believes in Him should not perish [mercy] but have everlasting life [grace]" (John 3:16).

When people appeal to the "character of God" to defend their view that no one should go to hell, they are missing the point. It is not God's fault that we all stand condemned by our own actions. God did not create a sinful, broken world. He created a perfect world, and we messed it up. Justice requires that the price be paid. Otherwise, God would not be God. God would not be reliable or trustworthy. It is only thanks to God that everyone is not in hell today! Because of His great love, He provided a remedy to the predicament we brought on ourselves. The great Princetonian theologian of the early twentieth century, Benjamin Warfield, put it this way, "The marvel of marvels is not that God, in his infinite love, has not elected all of this guilty race to be saved… What really needs accounting for—though to account for it passes the powers of our extremest flights of imagination—is how the holy God could get the consent of his nature to save a single sinner!"

One way to restate what we have been saying is this, "If anyone wants to go to hell, they can; but they don't have to." God has made it possible for anyone and everyone to receive mercy and grace. Still, unless you trust in Jesus Christ, and Him alone, as the only One who can save you, you will face justice. Justice must be served. There is no other option for an immutable God.

> **If anyone wants to go to hell, they can; but they don't have to.**

Freely Given, Freely Received

Why do some people go to hell when they die? Ultimately, there is only one reason: *unbelief.* If you do not believe the good news about Jesus, you will "die in your sins," as Jesus said (John 8:24). The message of salvation in Christ is universally offered to one and all. "For the grace of God that brings salvation has appeared to *all men*" (Titus 2:11). Jesus said, "Come to Me, *all* you who labor and are heavy laden, and I will give you rest" (Matthew 11:28). He said, "I am the bread of life; *whoever* comes to me shall not hunger, and *whoever* believes in me shall never thirst" (John 6:35, ESV).

The only means of receiving forgiveness of sins and eternal life is faith. "For God so loved the world that He gave His only begotten Son, that *whoever* believes in Him should not perish but have everlasting life" (John 3:16). Eternal salvation is freely offered, and it can only be freely received. We receive this free gift by faith alone in Christ alone, who died in substitutionary sacrifice for our sins and rose again. "Therefore being justified by faith, we have peace with God through our Lord Jesus Christ" (Romans 5:1, KJV).

The Bible tells us that Satan is blinding men's hearts to the Gospel (2 Corinthians 4:4), and the devil uses many avenues of deceit in convincing people to reject the free offer of forgiveness in Christ. Unbelief is the explosion, metaphorically speaking, that ultimately results in an eternity in hell. However, this explosion can be created by several different kinds of bombs. Why do some people choose not to believe the Gospel and end up in hell when they die? In more than thirty years of ministry, I have observed many reasons some people choose not to believe the Gospel and receive the free gift of salvation. In the remainder of this book I address some of these reasons.

For Further Discussion

1. What is the ultimate reason a person goes to hell instead of heaven?
2. When and how did sin enter the world?
3. What is the consequence of sin for individuals?

4. Is there anything a person can do to earn forgiveness apart from faith in Christ?

5. Explain this statement: "If you are born only once, you will die twice; but if you are born twice, you will die only once."

6. How did God remedy humankind's sin problem?

7. How do individuals personally receive the payment for sin that Christ made on our behalf?

8. What does it mean to be "born again"?

9. Define justice, mercy, and grace and explain their relationship to one another.

10. How does God's redemptive plan meet the requirements of justice, mercy, and grace?

2

Too Smart for Your Own Good

There is a principle which is a bar against all information, which is proof against all argument, and which cannot fail to keep a man in everlasting ignorance. This principle is contempt prior to examination.
—British theologian William Paley (1879)

Intelligence is no guarantee against making dumb decisions. Some of the smartest people in history have done really stupid things. There is even a support group for highly intelligent individuals who make incomprehensible blunders, invented by Mortimer R. Feinberg and John J. Tarrant. It is called *Smart Screwups Anonymous* (SSA). Members of SSA all share the same problem: They each messed up their lives by doing idiotic things that people as smart as them should have known better than to do. You might say they were "too smart for their own good."

According to David Robson, author of *The Intelligence Trap* (2019), people who are intelligent are actually significantly more at risk from certain kinds of biases in their judgment. "You might expect Nobel prizes to correlate positively with rational thinking," he writes, "but this is by no means automatic." Scientists and other smart people, it seems, are not always good at critical thinking. Robson says there is a word for the significant mismatch between intelligence and rational thinking: *dysrationalia*. An article by Heather Butler from *Scientific American* magazine in 2017 concurs with Robson's findings: "Intelligence is not the same as critical thinking—and the difference matters."

A lack of critical thinking is nothing new. We could go back thousands of years and find examples of smart people who arrived at seriously flawed conclusions. King David and King Solomon come to mind. Let us go back to the year 51 AD, however, and take a look at one prime example. It was early spring, and the Apostle Paul was in the midst of his second missionary journey (Acts 17). It had been a roller-coaster ride thus far. He had faced intense persecution in Thessalonica, narrowly escaping a riotous mob. From there he moved on to Berea, where his missionary endeavors were met with great success as the locals searched the Scriptures and carefully analyzed what Paul was saying. From Berea, Paul moved on to Athens.

The Athenian Philosophers

Athens was still the cultural and intellectual center of the Greek world at the time, even though its heyday had been centuries earlier. Looking around, Paul observed many temples and statues (some of which remain there today). In our day, these relics are of interest primarily for their historic and artistic values, but in Paul's day they were idols and objects of worship that the Greeks regarded as holy. William Barclay noted, "It was said that there were more statues of the gods in Athens than in all the rest of Greece put together, and that in Athens it was easier to meet a god than a man."

As Paul waited for Timothy and Silas to arrive, he reasoned in the synagogue and the marketplace with anyone who would listen. Athenian philosophers gathered in the marketplace, called the *agora*, to discuss and debate their views. This agora was west of the Acropolis, on which the remains of the Parthenon still stand today. The Acropolis of Athens is like a citadel—an ancient fortified area of the city—located on a rocky outcrop above the city. In addition to the Parthenon, the Acropolis contains the remains of several ancient buildings of great architectural and historic significance.

Paul's sermons eventually caught the attention of the city's intellectual elite, including some Epicurean and Stoic philosophers. Epicureans were followers of Epicurus (341–270 BC) who believed that pleasure was the ultimate goal of life. Such hedonistic thinking was common in the Greek schools of philosophy of the fourth century BC, and its impact was still felt in Paul's day. Epicurus taught that the gods were aloof to what was going on with humankind. Consequently, everything happens by chance and death is the end of it all. This philosophy is still popular today in many circles.

Stoics followed the teachings of Zeno the Cypriot (340–65 BC). The term *stoic* comes from the Greek word *stoa*, meaning "colonnade" or "portico." It refers to a large porch where Zeno taught during his time in Athens. His followers emphasized the importance of being one with nature. They stressed individuality, rationalism, and self-sufficiency. They were known for their high-mindedness and condescension. Stoics were pantheists; that is, they taught that reality is identical with divinity, or to put it more commonly, God is in everything and everything is God. They also believed that we have no power to influence the future or even our own actions—a view known as fatalism. Their teaching is also common today.

Having aroused the attention of the Epicureans and Stoics, Paul was summoned to Mars' Hill, a prominent rock outcropping located northwest of the Acropolis. The Greeks called this area the Areopagus, but it was known as Mars' Hill to the Romans. A group of about thirty notable citizens—a council of sorts—met there, and this group had authority over many aspects of daily life in Athens such as religion, morals, and education. They wanted to know what message Paul was pushing, because they thought what he was saying was peculiar (Acts 17:19).

They called Paul a "babbler" (literally, a "seed picker"). The Greek word translated as "babbler" (*spermologos*) is a metaphor referring to someone who picks up the words of others the way a bird picks up seeds. The implication was that Paul was cobbling together a new doctrine by picking up isolated ideas here and there from various sources. Paul's commanding style and appeal to the absolute authority of God's Word challenged the thinking of these philosophers. Years earlier, Socrates had been poisoned by his enemies for teaching strange ideas in Athens, so this was a tense situation. In front of this council of elites, Paul preached one of his most famous sermons.

In his sermon at Mars' Hill, Paul systematically refuted the arguments of the Athenian philosophers. He exposed them as being too smart for their own good when they rejected the good news about Jesus Christ. Two thousand years later, many people still make the same mistake. Some people end up in hell because their high-minded, philosophical ideas blind them to

> **Some people end up in hell because their high-minded, philosophical ideas blind them to the truth.**

the truth. They are simply unwilling to believe the plain, simple message of the Gospel. Let's take a closer look at how Paul countered the false wisdom of these erudite noblemen.

Relationship is more important than religion

The Athenians thought that life was all about religion. Their focus was on who or what you worshipped, how you worshipped, when you worshipped, and where you worshipped. It was all about a religious system. Paul explained that *religion* will not cut it. It is *relationship* that matters. Let's take a look at how he opened his sermon.

> Then Paul stood in the midst of the Areopagus and said, "Men of Athens, I perceive that in all things you are very religious; for as I was passing through and considering the

objects of your worship, I even found an altar with this inscription: TO THE UNKNOWN GOD Therefore, the One whom you worship without knowing, Him I proclaim to you" (Acts 17:22–23).

Paul was not placating his audience by calling them "very religious." He was simply stating a fact. There was no doubt that religion was central in the lives of the citizens of Athens. As was his custom, Paul sought to connect with his audience by meeting them where they were in their thinking. The Athenians were so religious that they even had altars to "unknown gods," lest they inadvertently leave out or offend some hidden deity. An altar from that era inscribed "To the Unknown Deities" has been uncovered in modern times at Pergamum (Pergamon), just across the Aegean Sea from Athens in what is now western Turkey. Archaeological discoveries such as this confirm the widespread religiosity of the ancient Greek culture.

Paul began by referencing the Athenians' interest in gods and their self-proclaimed ignorance about at least one god. He then proceeded to explain what the One True God, the Creator of the Universe, had revealed about Himself. He explained how anyone can have a relationship with the Creator. The Athenians were doing many well-intentioned things, but they were too smart for their own good. In their philosophical brilliance, they had overlooked the most basic element of life: relationship. For the same reason, many people today focus on the intellectual, academic aspect of religion to the exclusion of the relational aspect.

> **Many people today focus on the intellectual, academic aspect of religion to the exclusion of the relational aspect.**

Yet, faith or belief is not about religion. It is about relationship. Jesus told the religious leaders of His day, "Many will say to Me in that day, 'Lord, Lord, have we not ... done many wonders in Your name?' And then I will declare to them, 'I never knew you; depart from Me'" (Matthew 7:22–23). It is not about *what* or *how much* you know; it's about who you know. Jesus said, "I am the way, the truth, and the life. No one comes to the Father except through Me" (John 14:6).

The Creator is more powerful than the created

Paul made a second argument in this famous sermon. He appealed to logic to show that man-made idols are no match for an eternal God. In making his case, Paul masterfully pitted the Epicureans against the Stoics. Paul's sermon continued:

> God, who made the world and everything in it, since He is Lord of heaven and earth, does not dwell in temples made with hands. Nor is He worshiped with men's hands, as though He needed anything, since He gives to all life, breath, and all things (Acts 17:24–25).

First, he presented God as the Creator and appealed to the Epicureans' idea of God as being above the world. The true God created all things, Paul explained. Because He is Lord of heaven and earth, human buildings cannot contain Him. He is transcendent over all. He is sovereign and powerful and awesome and mighty. This corresponded with the Epicureans' idea of God's transcendency. The Epicureans would have been shouting a collective "Amen!" at this point. Meanwhile, the pantheistic Stoics (who thought everyone and everything was a god, even statues) would have been saying, "Wait just a minute!"

Having fired a few shots at the Stoics, Paul next took aim at the Epicureans' false view of truth. The true God, Paul insisted, sustains all things. He does not need people to sustain Him. In other words, He is immanent as well as transcendent. The Stoics understood God's immanence; they just overplayed it. God participates intimately in human existence, but that does not mean that every tree, or plant, or animal, or person is a god. This contradicted the Epicureans' belief that God took no interest in human affairs, and it sent a dagger through the heart of the Stoics' view of self-sufficiency. Either way, the point is that the Creator is more powerful than the created.

Perhaps more than anything else, this is what skeptics need to understand, both then and now. There is a God and you are not Him. He is powerful, just, holy, righteous, and sovereign; and He is equally loving, merciful, and gracious. Those who ignore Him do so at their own peril. Nothing humankind can do can take the place of God. "Our God is in heaven; He does whatever He pleases" (Psalm 115:3). As King David sang when the ark was brought into the tabernacle, "The LORD is great and greatly to be praised; He is also to be feared above all gods. For all the gods of the peoples are idols, but the LORD made the heavens" (1 Chronicles 16:25–26).

> **There is a God and you are not Him.**

Paul's argument is that you cannot have it both ways. You cannot claim that there is a powerful transcendent God, like the Epicureans did, while at the same time claiming to believe with the Stoics that God is some impotent spirit at the mercy of his subjects, a god who floats around and dwells in trees and man-made statues and is subject to his creation. This was a masterful argument that no doubt had the philosophers scratching their heads. About six years after Paul's interaction with the Athenians, he would write these words to the Romans: "Oh, the depth of the riches both of the wisdom and knowledge of God! How unsearchable are His judgments and His ways past finding out! ... For of Him and through Him and to Him are all things, to whom be glory forever. Amen" (Romans 11:33–36).

In his sermon at Mars' Hill, Paul was essentially echoing the words of the anonymous psalmist who said, "O LORD, how great are Your works! Your thoughts are very deep" (Psalm 92:5). In other words, God is a powerful Creator who is hard to comprehend. Yet, He is approachable and accessible and welcomes anyone, anytime, if that person will merely come to Him in faith. For millennia humankind has tried to usurp God's authority: whether it was the Nephilim in the days of Noah, the arrogant ideas promoted by those at the Tower of Babel, pagan kings like Nebuchadnezzar who demanded worldwide worship, the religious skeptics of Paul's day, or the brilliant minds of many today. No one can take the place of God. No one. Those who refuse to humble themselves, acknowledge their need for a Savior, and accept the free gift of forgiveness in Christ are too smart for their own good. Sadly, for this reason, many have ended up in hell.

No one can take the place of God.

God's plan is more reliable than man's philosophy
Paul's sermon continues with a third line of reasoning. These philosophical elitists thought that the Greeks were racially superior to all other people, and the Athenians were seen as the cream of the crop among the Grecians. Paul pointed out that they, like everyone else, had descended from one man, Adam. All of humanity shares one blood and is part of one race, the Adamic race. Therefore, no single ethnic group can claim to be better than another. Moreover, God has determined the time and place for all peoples. The nations are under His control, not their own. He is sovereign over their beginning and end, their boundaries, and their status in the world at large. God orders the political and military affairs of all nations. Although "the Greeks liked to think that they determined their own destiny," as Tom Constable put it, in reality God is in full control. Notice what Paul says:

> And He has made from one blood every nation of men to dwell on all the face of the earth, and has determined their

preappointed times and the boundaries of their dwellings, so that they should seek the Lord, in the hope that they might grope for Him and find Him, though He is not far from each one of us; for in Him we live and move and have our being, as also some of your own poets have said, "For we are also His offspring" (Acts 17:26–28).

In other words, God's plan is more reliable than man's philosophy. You can sit around the Areopagus all day, Paul says, pontificating and speculating and philosophizing, but that won't change who God is. He is sovereign. He knows what He is doing. He never looks down from heaven and declares, "I didn't see that coming!" God's active, visible role in the world is intended to draw people to Him as they acknowledge His sovereignty. In Romans, Paul reminds us that God's presence is

God's plan is more reliable than man's philosophy.

clearly seen in His creation (Romans 1:19–20). Similarly, David wrote, "The heavens declare the glory of God; and the firmament shows His handiwork" (Psalm 19:1). Nevertheless, throughout human history, many people have failed to find Him. This is often true of those who are wise and learned by the world's standard.

Sometimes intelligent, brilliant, philosophically minded people are too smart for their own good. "Just look around," Paul says. "How can you deny the existence of God?" God has revealed some knowledge of Himself and His will to all men through His creation. This general revelation, if recognized, will be clarified and illuminated by His special revelation through the Gospel. Paul continues his argumentation by quoting two Greek writers who would have been familiar to his educated audience. These writers, though not believers, expressed ideas that were consistent with what Paul had been saying.

The two poets that Paul quoted are Epimenides (ca. 600 BC) and Aratus (ca. 315–240 BC). Epimenides had written, "For in Thee we live and move and have our being." Aratus, as well as Cleanthes (331–233 BC), had written, "We are also his offspring." Paul was a master orator. His purpose in using these quotations was to get these intelligent philosophers to listen and (he hoped) agree with the point he was making: Namely, God has a plan and it trumps man's philosophy all day

> **It is worth noting that unbelievers are not always wrong.**

long. Paul shows that even worldly philosophers admitted this at times. It is worth noting that unbelievers are not always wrong.

God's command is more urgent than man's contemplation
Paul ended his sermon at Mars' Hill with one final point. His conclusion was that worshipping lifeless idols is irrational. God is the Creator of the universe. He is not some mere image or icon. You can almost see Paul pointing at the sculptures all around him. "How can these things create anything? Stop sitting around these idle idols and do what the Creator tells you to do," he insists. God's command is far more urgent than man's contemplation. Paul declares:

> Therefore, since we are the offspring of God, we ought
> not to think that the Divine Nature is like gold or silver
> or stone, something shaped by art and man's devising.
> Truly, these times of ignorance God overlooked, but now
> commands all men everywhere to repent, because He has
> appointed a day on which He will judge the world in righ-
> teousness by the Man whom He has ordained. He has given
> assurance of this to all by raising Him from the dead
> (Acts 17:29–31).

In this passage, Paul begins by telling the Athenians what they should not be doing (worshipping silly idols), and then proceeds to tell them what they should be doing: repenting. God is patient,

Paul explains. Before Jesus Christ came, people did not have as much revelation to respond to. They were still accountable to trust God, but they were ignorant of many of the truths about Him and His plan of redemption that we see clearly now. Essentially, Paul was saying to these philosophers, "I can understand how you might have missed God's plan for redemption in times past. But today, now that God has come in the flesh, how can you possibly miss Him?"

It was time for these intellectuals to repent. They had to change their minds about who God is and how they can be rescued from hell. The good news of the Gospel could not be any clearer. The Epicureans and Stoics needed to look past their own introspective musings and see the truth: Everyone is a sinner. The penalty for sin is eternity in a literal place of torment called hell. Christ paid the penalty for sin when He died and rose again. He offers the gift of forgiveness and eternal life to anyone who will trust in Him and Him alone for it. Sadly, some of the Athenian philosophers rejected Paul's message. Luke tells us, "When they heard of the resurrection of the dead, some mocked" (Acts 17:32). Voltaire was right, "It is difficult to free fools from the chains they revere."

Some of the philosophers did not outright reject the truth, but they put off making a decision. "We will hear you again on this matter," they said (Acts 17:32). Nevertheless, God's command is more urgent than man's contemplation. Notice that Paul did not close his message by saying "take all the time you need; keep contemplating; no rush." Rather, he referred to a coming day of judgment. God has "appointed a day on which He will judge

> **God's command is more urgent than man's contemplation.**

the world in righteousness by the Man whom He has ordained" (Acts 17:31). There is an urgency to the Gospel. Judgment day is coming. The time to believe is now.

This same message has echoed throughout the world for the last two thousand years. We are not as ignorant now as we once were. Christ has come. "God, who at various times and in various ways spoke in time past to the fathers by the prophets, has in these last days spoken to us by His Son" (Hebrews 1:1–2). The life, death, and resurrection of Christ are the most historically attested events in human history. God commands everyone everywhere to repent, change their mind about their idols and whatever false philosophies they think can save them, and believe in Jesus Christ. Don't be one of those people who ends up in hell because you were too smart for your own good!

For Further Discussion

1. Why do smart people sometimes make really dumb mistakes?

2. Can human intelligence be counted on to solve humankind's spiritual problem?

3. Who was Paul's audience at Mars' Hill?

4. Which is more important, *religion* or *relationship*? Why?

5. Explain the foolishness of worshipping man-made idols.

6. Would you rather rely on God's plan or your own philosophy?

7. Why is there an urgency to the Gospel message?

3
I'm OK – You're OK?

Those who are well have no need of a physician, but those who are sick. — Jesus Christ (Matthew 9:12)

Dr. Thomas A. Harris was a chief psychiatric officer with the Navy during World War II. In 1969, he published a book that changed the way people think about themselves and others — and not in a good way. Its message still reverberates loudly through the halls of humanistic psychology and psychiatry today. The book was titled *I'm OK — You're OK*, and it spent nearly two years on the New York Times Best Seller list. More than fifteen million copies have been sold, according to Harper & Row, Harris's publisher. *I'm OK—You're OK* has been translated into twenty-five languages.

The theories Harris proposed in his famous book were based upon ideas first developed by Dr. Eric Berne, called transactional analysis. Berne's book, *Games People Play* (1964), had a profound impact on Harris. According to Berne's transactional approach to psychology, there are four life positions that you can hold, and holding a particular psychological position has implications for how you function in life and interact with others. The four life positions are: (1) I'm OK—You're OK; (2) I'm OK—You're not OK; (3) I'm not OK—You're OK; and (4) I'm not OK—You're not OK. The "I'm OK—You're OK" position is allegedly the healthiest position about life, and helping people consistently operate from that position is the goal of secular psychotherapy.

There is one major problem with this approach: it directly contradicts what the Bible has to say about the nature of man. As discussed previously, humankind is born in sin—broken, corrupt, and in need of redemption—and only a relationship with Jesus Christ can help us become whole once again. Underlying Harris's model in *I'm OK—You're OK* is a Freudian approach to human nature and personality, according to which every human being starts out in the "I'm OK" position. Yet, according to Scripture, we are decidedly *not* OK from the moment of birth. We are depraved, and if this depravity is left unremedied it gets worse. Depravity does not get better over time, no matter how many self-help books we read or expensive therapy sessions we sit through. Depravity is a degenerative disease. Freudian psychology is an antibiblical paradigm.

Sigmund Freud, the father of psychoanalysis, was heavily influenced by the famous eugenicist Charles Darwin. Therefore, in order to understand the dangers of the "I'm OK You're OK" mentality, we must first take a look at the underlying principles of Darwinism. Contrary to what you might have learned from your seventh-grade biology textbook, Charles Darwin was not a scientist; he was a eugenicist. *Eugenics* is a belief system that aims to improve the genetic quality of the human population by killing and gradually weeding out people and groups that are judged to be inferior.

The little-known subtitle of Darwin's magnum opus, *Origin of the Species*, is *The Preservation of Favoured Races in the Struggle for Life*. According to Darwin, we are not all from one blood made in the image of God, as the Bible tells us; rather, some races are better than others. In his 1871 work *The Descent of Man*, Darwin wrote that most people are "evolutionary dead ends" and only a "small elite" is "actually evolving" and everyone else "just gets in the way" and ought to be eliminated. Man is generally good, Darwin believed, and those who aren't—the sick, lame, mentally ill, people of color, etc.—must be culled out before they corrupt the pure gene pool. It is worth noting that Darwin was Adolf Hitler's role model and hero. Voltaire warned, "Those who can make you believe absurdities can make you commit atrocities." Hitler is a case in point; he put into practice, on a horrific scale, Darwin's biological theories.

Just as Hitler applied Darwin's theories to politics and society, Freud applied Darwinism to the human psyche. Freud wrote that "the theories of Darwin ... strongly attracted me, for they held out hopes of extraordinary advance in our understanding of the world." Freud believed that the study of evolution was an essential part of the training to become a psychoanalyst. Thus, all modern psychiatrists are at least indirectly influenced by Darwinism, and this includes Thomas A. Harris, the author of *I'm OK — You're OK*.

Some people end up in hell because they have adopted this widespread, Freudian, humanistic view of reality in which they see themselves as perfectly fine. They are convinced they have no need of redemption or salvation. Their motto is, "If it ain't broke, don't fix it," and they do not realize that they are broken. In light of Satan's ceaseless efforts to blind men's hearts to the gospel (2 Corinthians 4:4), it should not surprise us that so many people are oblivious to their

> **Before a person will reach for the life-preserver, he must first realize he is drowning; and before a person will seek forgiveness, he must first realize he is a sinner who needs a Savior.**

own condition. Lewis Sperry Chafer elaborates on this reality:

> It is not strange that the wise and cultured of this world feel their aesthetic natures shocked by the blood of the Cross, yet entertain no sense of their own abhorrent pollution in the sight of the infinitely holy One. It is not strange that

the world assumes to have advanced beyond that which is repeatedly said to be the manifestation of the wisdom of God; branding as bigots, insincere, or ignorant, all who still hold to the whole testimony of God. It is not strange that the atonement by blood is omitted, for it is Satan's hour and the power of darkness, and the true child of God must patiently bear the ever-increasing reproaches of his crucified Lord, until the glory dawns and the shadows flee away.

Before a person will reach for the life-preserver, he must first realize he is drowning; and before a person will seek forgiveness, he must first realize he is a sinner who needs a Savior. Jesus said, "Those who are well have no need of a physician, but those who are sick" (Luke 5:31).

The Rich Young Ruler

The reality that some people refuse to believe the Gospel because they don't realize they have a problem is nothing new. This thinking has been around since time began. Consider the example of the rich young ruler in Jesus' day.

Now behold, one came and said to Him, "Good Teacher, what good thing shall I do that I may have eternal life?" So He said to him, "Why do you call Me good? No one is good but One, that is, God. But if you want to enter into life, keep the commandments." He said to Him, "Which ones?" Jesus said, "'You shall not murder,' 'You shall not commit adultery,' 'You shall not steal,' 'You shall not bear false witness,' 'Honor your father and your mother,' and, 'You shall love your neighbor as yourself'" (Matthew 19:16–19).

Like most people do from time to time, this young man was contemplating eternal life. He undoubtedly had heard the chatter among people around town about "the Kingdom of Heaven" being at hand and it caused him to wonder, "Where will I spend eternity?" There are a variety of reasons that heaven might cross someone's mind. It might be the loss of a loved one; perhaps she attended a funeral; perhaps he watched a movie in which death played a central role. It is not uncommon for something to trigger thoughts about the afterlife. Notice that this young man thought he must "do" something to earn his place in heaven. We will say more about this in chapter 5.

Jesus answers the man's question by pointing him to the commandments. Jesus essentially says, "If you keep the commandments, you're in!" This is the same message Jesus preached in the Sermon on the Mount. If you want to go to heaven when you die, you must "be perfect, just as your Father in heaven is perfect" (Matthew 5:48). The righteousness that heaven demands is *perfect* righteousness. It is an all-or-nothing scenario. God does not grade on a curve. Either you pass or you fail; and to pass, you must be perfect. Either you keep all the commandments; or you may as well have broken them all. "For whoever shall keep the whole law, and yet stumble in one point, he is guilty of all" (James 2:10).

The sinfulness of Adam is imputed to every human being. That is, it is charged to our account. "Therefore, as through one man's offense judgment came to all men, resulting in condemnation" (Romans 5:18a). When we believe the Gospel, because of our faith, the perfect righteousness of Christ is imputed to us. We are "justified by faith" (Romans 5:1). "God was in Christ reconciling the world to Himself, not imputing their trespasses to them" (2 Corinthians 5:19). "Even so through one Man's righteous act the free gift came to all men, resulting in justification of life" (Romans 5:18b). "For as in Adam all die, even so in Christ all shall be made alive" (1 Corinthians 15:22). "For He made Him who knew no sin to be sin for us, that we might become the righteousness of God in Him" (2 Corinthians 5:21).

When the young man heard Jesus' response, he thought he was in great shape. "I'm OK!" he concluded. Notice what he said, "All these things I have kept from my youth. What do I still lack?" (Matthew 19:20). The rich young ruler thought he had it covered. He did not acknowledge his sin. Like many of the religious elites of his day, he thought he had dotted all of his I's and crossed all of his T's. However, Jesus says, "Not so fast."

Knowing what the young man was thinking, Jesus said to him, "If you want to be perfect, go, sell what you have and give to the poor, and you will have treasure in heaven; and come, follow Me" (Matthew 19:21). Jesus implied that the man was not, in fact, perfect, and He zeroed in on one aspect of the Law that this young man had neglected: benevolence. The rich young ruler had forgotten about Jewish laws that commanded compassion for the poor. He had forgotten, for example, the Law of Moses in Deuteronomy 15.

> If there is among you a poor man of your brethren, within any of the gates in your land which the Lord your God is giving you, you shall not harden your heart nor shut your hand from your poor brother …. For the poor will never cease from the land; therefore, I command you, saying, "You shall open your hand wide to your brother, to your poor and your needy, in your land" (Deuteronomy 15:7–11).

When the young man heard this, he "went away sorrowful" (Matthew 19:22). He apparently understood at that moment that he had a problem. He knew that he had to keep all of the Law if he wanted to go to heaven, yet his discussion with Jesus had reminded him that he was far from perfect. There is no evidence the rich young ruler ever believed the Gospel. This encounter illustrates a key reason some people spend eternity in hell. They think they are "OK" and have no need for a Savior.

Whatever Happened to Sin?

This faulty "I'm OK" mentality is pervasive in many churches today. Sin is redefined as a "weakness," "flaw," "limitation," "imperfection," "shortcoming," "mistake," or "insecurity." For example, Joel Osteen, one of the most popular evangelical preachers of our day, told Larry King, "I don't use [the word sinners] ... Most people already know what they're doing wrong. When I get them to church I want to tell them that you can change... I don't go down the road of condemning." In his first best-selling book, *Your Best Life Now*, Osteen declares, "God focuses on the things you're doing right. He sees the best in you. ...you can stop obsessing about all your faults and give yourselves a break. Every person has weaknesses." By his own admission, Osteen goes to great effort to avoid using the word *sin*.

Osteen is not alone. These days, personal responsibility and guilt are overlooked everywhere you turn. Commenting on this tendency, D. A. Carson laments, "[In] our efforts to make Jesus appear relevant we have cast the human dilemma in merely contemporary categories, taking our cues from the perceived needs of our day." Colin Smith put it this way, "For most people in our society, the word *sin* has been emptied of its true meaning and filled with another meaning that renders it harmless." It is difficult to fathom how we can present the Gospel without addressing the sinfulness of mankind. Indeed, sin is the crux of the matter when it comes to salvation. Yet this is precisely what many contemporary preachers and theologians do, with devastating results. We have raised a generation of people who think they are OK. So, why should they believe the Gospel?

> **These days, personal responsibility and guilt are overlooked everywhere you turn.**

God's plan of salvation, by its nature, demands that we understand sin and its penalty. The grand metanarrative of human history goes from creation to corruption to redemption. If we leave out the *corruption* part, there is no need for salvation. The word "save" in Scripture (Gk. *sodzo*; Heb. *yasha*) means "rescue" or "deliver." It is a transitive verb, meaning it requires an object. Save does not exist in a vacuum. It must have content. Saved *from what*? Delivered *from what*? Rescued *from what*?

> **God's plan of salvation, by its nature, demands that we understand sin and its penalty.**

The answer is the penalty of sin: namely, eternity in hell. The fall of humankind did not result merely in a less enjoyable life on Earth. The consequences of sin are not only physical and temporal, but also eternal. The ultimate fate of those who do not believe the Gospel is a place of eternal torment. "Anyone not found written in the Book of Life was cast into the lake of fire" (Revelation 20:15).

> **The consequences of sin are not only physical and temporal, but also eternal.**

Fire Insurance? Yes!

Because of the prevalent disinterest in sin and hell these days, a new refrain has made its way into the mainstream Christian dialogue. I have heard it myself many times. Someone will say something like, "If the only reason you are believing the Gospel is to avoid hell, it does not count. Salvation is not simply fire insurance!" To those with that perspective, I say respectfully, "That's precisely what salvation is—fire insurance."

Christ did *not* die on the cross so that people would be happier, healthier, wealthier, or better in the here and now. He did *not* die on the cross so that we would feel more content, have a positive outlook, or live our best life now. Lewis Sperry Chafer correctly notes, "Christ did not die to show us how to die; He died that we might not die." In other words, He did not die so that we could be successful in our earthly lives and end well. He died to pay our personal penalty for sin and guarantee that we could avoid an eternity in hell. Jesus warned that those who do not believe in Him will "die in their sins" (John 8:24) and spend eternity in "the everlasting fire prepared for the devil and his angels" (Matthew 25:41). They will be cast into the "furnace of fire," where there will be "wailing and gnashing of teeth" (Matthew 13:42).

Why are so many people bothered by the notion that salvation is about being rescued from hell? It seems plain enough from Scripture that this is the case. As mentioned earlier, people are hung up over the so-called "fire insurance" idea of salvation because the very concepts of hell and sin have been marginalized in popular culture. There is a second reason, however, that some are concerned about salvation being presented in terms of avoiding hell. Among conservative Christians — that is, those who believe the Bible is the only standard for our beliefs — there are a growing number who believe that salvation is about what we do, or promise to do, for God more than what God offers us. To them, your motive in seeking salvation matters more than salvation itself. Where did this idea originate, and why has it become entrenched in the theological worldview of so many Christians?

"I hereby solemnly swear…"
This perspective has developed due to the pervasive spread of a particular brand of theology in Christian circles today, especially among Gen-Xers, Millennials, and even some teenagers and college students. Known as Reformed theology, this viewpoint is by no means new; it has been around in some form or fashion since the days of the Reformation. However,

over the past few decades it has gained enormous momentum in the minds of many Christians because of influential teachers such as John Piper, John MacArthur, R. C. Sproul, Albert Mohler, James Montgomery Boice, J. I. Packer, and others. While I respect these biblical scholars, I have an honest and earnest disagreement with them about the nature of salvation.

According to Reformed teaching, in order to receive eternal salvation, you must first make a pledge or commitment to God promising to forsake all of your sins and follow Him faithfully. This pledge or commitment is part and parcel of faith, they say. Thus, they defend the notion of *sola fide* (faith alone) as the cry of the Reformation — which it was. However, they have redefined "faith" to include a component that is not inherent in the meaning of the word. Faith, they insist, must include a personal commitment to God or it is not real faith. This component of a commitment or pledge is what they call *fiducia*.

Consider the following statement from John MacArthur. "Faith is not true faith if it lacks *fiducia*," which he defines as "an attitude of surrender to Christ's authority." R. C. Sproul describes *fiducia* as a necessary component of saving faith that involves believing that the Gospel is "not only true, but also … most worthy of our love and desire." J. I. Packer likewise insists that *fiducia* is a required part of faith if you are to be saved. He defines *fiducia* as "whole-souled response involving mind, heart, will, and affections," and a change of heart that "desires holiness."

In other words, according to this view, it is not enough merely to believe that Jesus Christ, the Son of God, died and rose again to pay your personal penalty for sin. If you really want to be saved, they say, you must surrender your whole self to Christ's authority, change your affections and will, and desire to be holy. John MacArthur, for example, writes, "The saving faith in Jesus Christ that the New Testament teaches is much more than a simple affirmation of certain truths about Him. … Saving faith is *a placing of oneself totally in submission to the Lord Jesus Christ… .*" Elsewhere, MacArthur writes, "The gospel call to faith presupposes that sinners must *repent of their sin and yield to Christ's authority.*"

One proponent of this view goes so far as to compare the salvation experience to a wedding ceremony in which two parties make a mutual agreement with one another. James Montgomery Boice uses an extended marriage metaphor to explain that eternal life is imparted only when Jesus and the would-be convert exchange vows. He even provides a suggested vow for the would-be convert to make: "I, sinner, take thee, Jesus, to be my Savior and Lord; and *I do promise and covenant,* before God and these witnesses, to be thy loving and faithful disciple." In this way, the salvation experience becomes nothing more than a contractual agreement based upon one's pledge of obedience rather than a free gift based upon faith alone in Christ alone.

No Strings Attached

The idea that faith, in order to impart eternal life, must include a willingness to surrender everything to God and follow Him faithfully reduces salvation to a bilateral contract, rather than the unilateral gift that the Bible says it is. Additionally, it presupposes that a person can comprehensively know all of his sins, motives, and shortcomings at the moment of salvation—knowledge that is impossible for the human mind to ascertain. Most importantly, though, such teaching contradicts the plain teaching of Scripture according to which salvation comes as a *free gift.* "The free gift of God is eternal life in Christ Jesus our Lord" (Romans 6:23,

> **If a gift comes with certain obligations, expectations, or requirements, it is no longer a "gift" but an "agreement." If it is not free, it is not grace.**

NASB). *Free*, by definition, means no strings attached. If a gift comes with certain obligations, expectations, or requirements, it is no longer a "gift" but an "agreement." The essence of the grace of God is that it is free. If it is not free, it is not grace. If we could bring something to the table to convince God to save us, Jesus would not have had to die in our place on the cross. The nineteenth-century hymn writer Elvina Hall had it right: "Jesus paid it all."

Salvation is not a fifty–fifty equation where we contribute something and God contributes something. Yet, astonishingly, that is exactly what Reformed theology teaches. MacArthur states unambiguously, "Salvation for sinners cost God His own Son; it cost God's Son His life, and *it'll cost you the same thing*." How can something that is *free* cost us something? "The free gift of God is eternal life in Christ Jesus our Lord (Romans 6:23, NASB). We are "justified freely by His grace through the redemption that is in Christ Jesus" (Romans 3:24). "Through one Man's righteous act the free gift came to all men, resulting in justification of life" (Romans 5:18). Jesus did not pay for most of our salvation, He paid for *all* of it!

God does not grant us forgiveness and eternal life on the basis of what we do or promise to do for Him. Yet this is precisely what MacArthur, and many others of his theological persuasion, insist. MacArthur states that it is not enough to "know and understand and assent to the facts of the gospel" and believe that "these truths apply to me personally" unless you also

> **God does not grant us forgiveness and eternal life on the basis of what we do or promise to do for Him.**

"shun sin" and "submit to the Lord Jesus." He suggests that a person who holds "that kind of belief" (i.e., belief without a pledge or promise) is "not guaranteed eternal life."

For those who insist that faith must include a pledge or promise to obey (and an attempt to do so), the idea that a person would trust in Christ simply to avoid the eternal consequences of sin—eternity in hell—is unacceptable. Your motive in seeking salvation cannot be self-serving, they say. You must be submissive and subservient. Christ does not save helpless sinners looking for redemption. He only saves those who are willing to reform themselves—or so some theologians tell us. However, true moral reform is not possible for an unbeliever and is never a test for the salvation of those who are saved "by grace through faith, not by works" (Ephesians 2:8–9).

One serious problem with this view is that it makes assurance of salvation impossible. It calls into question the very words of Christ when He says to those who believe in Him, "I give you eternal life and you shall never perish" (John 10:28). It casts doubt on the plain meaning of Jesus' words, "Most assuredly, I say to you, he who believes in Me has everlasting life" (John 6:47). Did Jesus mean what He said? Or did He really mean, "Most likely, if you keep your promise and follow Me faithfully, you might

> **Every believer, from the moment he places his faith in Jesus Christ for salvation, can be assured of his eternal home in heaven.**

have eternal life"? I believe Jesus meant what He said and that every believer, from the moment he places his faith in Jesus Christ for salvation, can be assured of his eternal home in heaven.

No Doubt about It!

The Bible tells us, "These things I have written to you who believe in the name of the Son of God, that you may *know* that you have eternal life" (1 John 5:13). Reformed theology not only engenders a lack of assurance among believers, it celebrates it. One leading Reformed theologian, Os Guinness, states plainly that it is healthy for Christians to doubt their eternal salvation. He says, "I believe in doubt," and insists that doubt can "strengthen faith." The premise that doubt somehow strengthens faith is puzzling, to say the least. Doubt, by definition, is the *absence of belief.* Belief and disbelief in the same object cannot coexist simultaneously. You can believe one thing and doubt something else at the same time, but you cannot believe and doubt the same thing simultaneously. Therefore, to suggest that doubt fosters assurance is a bit like suggesting that heat strengthens ice, or light strengthens darkness.

Doubt and assurance are mutually exclusive—they do not help one another. If they did help one another, then the best remedy for a lack of faith would be more doubt! This could lead to ridiculous implications. When someone comes to you expressing doubt about his or her salvation, following this line of reasoning, you should counsel the person, "If you want to have assurance that you are saved, keep doubting your salvation. The more you doubt, the more sure you will become because doubt strengthens your faith!" The whole idea is absurd.

The Bible certainly does not teach that believers should doubt their salvation. Pastor Adrian Rogers once commented, "Worry is a mild form of atheism"; so too is doubting our salvation once we have it. To doubt the promise of Jesus Christ is a sin. It would be like saying to Him, "I know You promised me eternal life if I simply believe in You for it, but I don't believe You." Yet, as Lewis Sperry Chafer correctly points out, "This one word 'believe' represents all a sinner can do and all a sinner must do

> **The Bible certainly does not teach that believers should doubt their salvation.**

to be saved." Chafer reminds us that faith is a simple concept. To add elements of so-called *fiducia* to the plain meaning of faith in Scripture is to distort it and confuse it. Chafer puts it eloquently:

> It is quite possible for any intelligent person to know whether he has placed such confidence in the Savior. Saving faith is a matter of personal consciousness. "I know whom I have believed." To have deposited one's eternal welfare in the hands of another is a decision of the mind so definite that it can hardly be confused with anything else. On this deposit of oneself into His saving grace depends one's eternal destiny.

Faith alone saves, not faith plus surrender, commit, promise, pledge, or anything else. When you recognize that you are a sinner, and that only Jesus Christ can forgive you and give you eternal life, you will come to Him in simple faith and freely receive the gift He has freely offered.

I'm Not OK You're Not OK

The false notion that saving faith requires a commitment to obey and follow Christ plays right into the hand of the *I'm OK—You're OK*, secular, self-help psychology. Notwithstanding its widespread popularity, this viewpoint is dangerous, because it suggests that whatever your limitations, weaknesses, flaws, or insecurities may be, you can overcome them simply by trying harder. Scripture, by contrast, is clear that only Jesus Christ can solve humankind's sin problem. "For there is one God and one Mediator between God and men, the Man Christ Jesus" (1 Timothy 2:5). Jesus said, "I am the way, the truth, and the life. No one comes to the Father except through Me" (John 14:6).

A more accurate title for a book about human nature would be *I'm NOT OK—You're NOT OK*. We are all sinners in need of a Savior. "For all have sinned and fall short of the glory of God"

(Romans 3:23). Jesus said, "If you do not believe that I am He, you will die in your sins" (John 8:24). Are you OK? You are if you have trusted in Jesus Christ and Him alone for salvation. Otherwise, no; you are not OK. Some people will end up in hell because they think they are OK and have no need of salvation. They do not understand that they desperately need a Savior, and His name is Jesus Christ.

***

For Further Discussion

1. What did Jesus mean when He said you must be perfect to get into heaven?
2. How can we become perfect?
3. Are people born essentially good, and become bad due to the influence of society? Or are we all born sinful, with a depraved nature?
4. When we receive salvation from God, what exactly are we being saved from?
5. Is our eternal salvation absolutely free, or must each of us bring something to the table?
6. Can I be sure that I will spend eternity in heaven when I die? Or must I wait until I die to find out?
7. Why is the *I'm OK—You're OK* philosophy so dangerous?

4
You Say Tomato

There is a way that seems right to a man, but its end is the way of death. — Proverbs 14:12

The movie *Shall We Dance*, starring Fred Astaire and Ginger Rogers, was released in 1937. It featured a score written by George Gershwin with lyrics written by Ira Gershwin, George's brother. Aside from its acclaim as one of ten films starring the famous Astaire/Rogers duo, *Shall We Dance* also had a lasting impact for its hit song, "Let's Call the Whole Thing Off." The song is number thirty-four on the American Film Institute's top 100 songs in American cinema of the twentieth century. Even if you are unfamiliar with the movie, you probably have heard the song's famous refrain:

> You say *eether* and I say *eyether*,
> You say *neether* and I say *nyther*;
> Eether, eyether, neether, nyther,
> Let's call the whole thing off!
> You like *potato* and I like *potahto*,
> You like *tomato* and I like *tomahto*;
> Potato, *potahto*, tomato, *tomahto*!
> Let's call the whole thing off!

Over the years, this celebrated chorus has morphed into the truncated phrase "tomayto tomahto" as an expression meaning "insignificant difference." When two people disagree about something that is deemed unimportant, one of them might say, "Tomayto tomahto." The idea conveyed is "What's the difference?" In this contemporary era where people are prone to draw circles of inclusion more than lines of distinction—an age where political correctness discourages people from expressing dogmatic conclusions—the phrase "tomayto tomahto" has become almost axiomatic. Are there any differences worth standing up for anymore?

This sentiment has had a significant impact on Christian theology. With no recognized authority for ultimate truth, every Christian has become an "expert" in the field of systematic theology. Doctrines once thought to be foundational standards of orthodoxy are now dismissed by tin-pot theologians as inconsequential or pointless. Substantive theological debates that occupied the minds of Christians in previous generations have given way to a "can't-we-all-just-get-along" mentality. This is true even of vital doctrines such as the doctrine of salvation.

Often when I explain to people that personal faith in Jesus is the only way to heaven, I am met with, "That's just your opinion," or "That's just one way to look at it." Someone has said that intellectual reasoning today is "all signpost and no destination … all flight path and no landing strip." No one wants to stand for anything. It takes real courage to defend truth in today's world, because you are likely to be standing alone. The essence of a lack of courage is the failure to stand for something. As Jim Hightower put it, in classic Texas politician style, "The opposite of courage is not cowardice. It is conformity. Even a dead fish can go with the flow."

Without a firm stake in the ground, every viewpoint is perceived as equally valid. This is a philosophical concept known as *pluralism*. D. A. Carson has written a monumental work on the influence of pluralistic thinking on the present culture, entitled *The Gagging of God: Christianity Confronts Pluralism*. In it, he defines pluralism as "the view that all religions have the same moral and spiritual value, and offer the same potential for achieving salvation, however 'salvation' may be construed." Carson describes what he calls "radical" pluralism as a "stance [which] holds that no religion can advance any legitimate claim to superiority over any other religion." He goes on to describe how a not-so-subtle form of pluralism has crept into Christianity. "This stance," Carson says, "while affirming the truth of fundamental Christian claims, nevertheless insists that God has revealed himself, even in saving ways, in other religions. Inclusivists normally contend that God's definitive act of self-disclosure is in Jesus Christ, and that he is in some way central to God's plan of salvation for the human race, but that salvation itself is available in other religions."

Pluralism, no matter how blatant or how subtle, is contrary to the plain teaching of God's Word. The Bible, by its own self-proclamation, makes Christianity the only pathway to heaven. The plain teaching about the exclusivity of Christ in the Bible stands unmistakably opposed to an inclusive view of truth. As mentioned previously, "There is one God and *one Mediator* between God and men, the Man Christ Jesus" (1 Timothy 2:5). Jesus said, "I am the way, the truth, and the life. *No one* comes to the Father *except through Me*" (John 14:6). Referring to Jesus Christ, Peter proclaimed, "Nor is there salvation in any other, for there is *no other name* under heaven given among men by which we must be saved" (Acts 4:12).

> **Pluralism, no matter how blatant or how subtle, is contrary to the plain teaching of God's Word.**

Some people go to hell when they die because they reject the biblical teaching that personal faith in Jesus is the only way to heaven. They may recognize their sinfulness and need for salvation. They may even believe that Jesus existed, died, and rose again. Yet, they view the specific means of obtaining salvation as if it were a buffet line at a cafeteria. Everyone gets to choose what they want (inclusivism) as long as they are sincere. They think that faith in *something* ... *anything* ... will open the doors of heaven as long as that faith is genuinely heartfelt. A Muslim's faith in the five pillars of Islam is good enough to get him into paradise, they say. A Buddhist's quest for nirvana is his own personal pathway to heaven, they say. A Hindu's understanding of reincarnation is just his version of eternal life, they say. It's all just "tomayto tomahto."

> ## Some people go to hell when they die because they reject the biblical teaching that personal faith in Jesus is the only way to heaven.

Kaleidoscope or Microscope?

This prevailing worldview in our culture today, often described as postmodern, or more recently post-Christian, encourages ambiguity and celebrates diversity. It rejects anything that is certain or absolute. Indeed, the more open-minded you are, the more intellectual you are thought to be. As rock legend Frank Zappa once put it, "A mind is like a parachute; it doesn't work if it is not open," and no one wants to dive into the intellectual arena without the accepted safeguard of tolerance in place. *Anything goes. Everyone is entitled to their opinion. Let's just agree to disagree.* These are the battle cries reverberating from the current ideological battlefield, and the rejection of the exclusivity of Christ in salvation represents a primary reason that some people end up in hell when they die.

Is there absolute truth? Is there only one way to heaven? Is the Bible our only standard for truth? Questions like these cut to the heart of the matter. Paul R. Shockley summarizes the dominant mindset of our day as a framework marked by the belief that "absolute or objective truth does not exist. What is true for one individual may not be true for another; and therefore, 'reality is in the mind of the beholder.'" Accordingly, "there is no objective, universal authority." This creates a unique and thorny obstacle in the search for eternal salvation.

If, as Shockley writes, "what is true for one individual may not be true for another," then each solution to humankind's sin problem is allowed to stand on its own even though it may contradict another. Worse, even two substantially similar presentations of the plan of salvation may be interpreted differently by the listener or reader, since "reality is in the mind of the beholder." In the absence of absolute standards, there is no basis on which to police the accuracy or meaning of any message that purports to provide eternal salvation. The realm of acceptability is broad—and growing broader all the time. The "gospel" in our day may be described as a *kaleidoscopic* gospel, emphasizing a shifting variety and diversity of content, rather than a *microscopic* Gospel, with its emphasis on precision, detail, and biblical accuracy.

The Certainty of Certainty

It is fashionable today, even among Christians, to be more welcoming and embracing of opposing viewpoints. The so-called experts tell us we will be more influential and well-liked if we avoid offending others. The hesitancy on the part of many Christians to espouse the concept of absolute certainty is commonplace. It shows just how much the world's philosophy has influenced Christian theology in our day. D. James Kennedy was

> **The timeless principles of God's Word are not subject to the dominant attitudes and whims of culture.**

correct when he pointed out that these days we are "learning more and more about everything, and yet we seem to know less and less for sure." It makes me wonder how such an ideology might have altered Job's famous proclamation, "For I know that my Redeemer lives, and He shall stand at last on the earth" (Job 19:25). If Job lived in our day perhaps he would have said, "I am seventy-five percent sure that my Redeemer lives."

As discussed previously, the Bible declares itself within its own pages to be true, pure, and right. The timeless principles of God's Word are not subject to the dominant attitudes and whims of culture. "The entirety of Your Word is *truth*, and every one of Your righteous judgments *endures forever*" (Psalm 119:160). "Therefore all Your precepts concerning all things I consider to be *right*" (Psalm 119:128). "Every Word of God is *pure*" (Proverbs 30:5). "*Forever*, O Lord, Your word is *settled* in heaven" (Psalm 119:89). "Concerning Your testimonies, I have known of old that You have founded them *forever*" (Psalm 119:152). These are not mealy-mouthed proclamations that smack of hesitancy or uncertainty; they are authoritative, confident, and bold. One of the stated goals of God's Word is for us to know the "certainty of the words of truth" (Proverbs 22:21).

If nothing can be known with certainty, how can anything be known at all? There is a certain certainty to certainty. When we express uncertainty about truth it only serves to undermine confidence in the one and only solution to humankind's sin problem. The fact that competing worldviews are all seen as equally valid discourages people from trusting in Jesus Christ as the only One who can forgive sin and give eternal life. Nevertheless, when it comes to how to have eternal life, the matter is settled. There is only one way.

> **There is a certain certainty to certainty.**

Since the Fall in the Garden of Eden, humankind has been trying to find a solution to its predicament. Even though God's plan of salvation has been readily available to and easily seen by all of creation, the tendency of the depraved nature is to seek to fill this spiritual void in unhealthy ways. In the words of country singer Johnny Lee, people often find themselves "looking for love in all the wrong places." The Bible concurs: "To the hungry soul every bitter thing is sweet" (Proverbs 27:7). Man's quest to fill his hungry soul has taken many forms over the years. When there is no single answer, many answers will inevitably arise. We can go back more than one thousand years before Christ to learn a lesson about the dangers of embracing a pluralistic view of truth.

> **When there is no single answer, many answers will inevitably arise.**

Choose You This Day!

The year was 1370 BC, and the Israelites had crossed the Jordan into Canaan some thirty-five years earlier. Joshua was nearing death, so he assembled the people to deliver one final challenge. Human nature is universal, and the culture in Joshua's day was in many ways no different than our own. Although God had warned them about equivocating as to the absolute truth of the Law and adopting the practices and beliefs of false religions in the region, the Israelites had quickly succumbed to the allure of curious new pagan rituals. They became enamored by the "gods," rather than remaining firmly devoted to the One True God—Yahweh. Listen to Joshua's admonition:

> Now therefore, fear the Lord, serve Him in sincerity and in truth, and put away the gods which your fathers served on the other side of the River and in Egypt. Serve the Lord! And if it seems evil to you to serve the Lord, choose for yourselves this day whom you will serve, whether the gods which your fathers served that were on the other side of the River, or the gods of the Amorites, in whose land you dwell. But as for me and my house, we will serve the Lord. (Joshua 24:14–15)

There was only one right answer to the challenge Joshua set before the people. As Don Campbell put it, "There could be no mixing of allegiance to God with idol-worship. A firm choice had to be made then as in every generation. People must choose between expediency and principle, between this world and eternity, between God and idols." The Bible calls people of all time to "turn to God from idols to serve the living and true God" (1 Thessalonians 1:9).

The Idol of Hesitation

The prevailing winds of uncertainty about truth in our culture have created a new idol: the idol of *hesitation*. This "tomayto tomahto" mentality is actually just another way of saying, "This issue does not really matter, so there is no urgency to it." The devil has blinded the hearts of people to the Gospel by convincing them that there is really no single, authoritative gospel at all. Anything goes. Thus, people think they can take their time; look around a bit; linger at the buffet line to make sure they choose something that is really to their liking. "You say chicken-fried steak; I say baked cod."

The problem is that you cannot stand in the buffet line forever. We are all headed for the end of the line someday where we will pay for whatever choice we make. "It is appointed for men to die once, but after this the judgment" (Hebrews 9:27). One of the consequences of underemphasizing sin, as discussed in chapter 3, as well as of the abandonment of certainty that is the focus of this present chapter, is a lessening of the urgency surrounding eternal damnation. The "what difference does it make?" mentality fails to create a decisive sense of crisis or exigency.

Moreover, because the ideology of the day is characterized by "decision making on the ethical bases of feelings, emotions, and impressions," as Paul Shockley suggests, many people seem content to *feel their way* to salvation no matter how long it takes. Most evangelical churches these days worship the idol of hesitation. They have adopted a decidedly nonthreatening approach to evangelism. Rather than presenting the pure Gospel and challenging the hearer to respond to it, preachers are more likely to give the lost person a comfortable period of time for personal reflection. Commenting on this lack of urgency, Ajith Fernando writes,

> Traditionally, Christians have been motivated to evange-lism through their belief that the gospel is absolutely true and is the only hope for salvation. However, the aptness of thinking in such categories as "absolutely true" and "only hope for salvation" is being questioned by today's plural-istic thinking. The postmodern mood is thus hostile to the idea of urgency as it is portrayed in the Bible.

In a "tomayto tomahto" world, there is no definitive line drawn in the sand whereby a lost person is warned of the eternal consequences of sin and its singular solution through faith alone in Christ alone. There is no urgency, no sense that "today might be the day" or "what if I died today?"

Let's Call the Whole Thing Off!

Faced with so many choices in the search for eternal life, some people become intellectually paralyzed, unable or unwilling to make a decision. Sensing no urgency, and confused by the options, they do nothing. Like Fred Astaire and Ginger Rogers, they cry out, "Let's call the whole thing off!" Sadly, this indecision means they end up in hell because they never believed the Gospel.

It should be remembered, however, that indecision is actually a choice; it is a choice to do nothing, which means that your sin problem remains unremedied. The choice to do nothing may seem like an acceptable decision in this pluralistic age where anything goes, but the Bible reminds us, "There is a way that seems right to a man, but its end is the way of death" (Proverbs 14:12). There is an urgency to the Gospel message. Jesus said, "If you do not believe that I am He, you will die in your sins" (John 8:24). "Behold, now is the accepted time; behold, now is the day of salvation" (2 Corinthians 6:2). James reminds us of the fleeting nature of life:

> **Faced with so many choices in the search for eternal life, some people become intellectually paralyzed, unable or unwilling to make a decision.**

> Come now, you who say, "Today or tomorrow we will go to such and such a city, spend a year there, buy and sell, and make a profit"; whereas you do not know what will happen tomorrow. For what is your life? It is even a vapor that appears for a little time and then vanishes away. Instead you ought to say, "If the Lord wills, we shall live and do this or that." (James 4:13–15)

It has been said, "He who hesitates is lost." This centuries-old maxim has eternal ramifications when it comes to believing the Gospel. When the Gospel is no longer articulated as the only solution to humankind's serious, eternal problem, but rather merely one option among many, it leads people to put off the decision to trust Christ for another day, like they do with other presumed unimportant decisions. For this reason, some people end up in hell.

For Further Discussion

1. Is there more than one way to get to heaven?
2. What is pluralism? Does the Bible support a pluralistic view of truth?
3. Is truth knowable?
4. Are there absolutes? Are there some things that are true for all people at all times?
5. How does a lack of certainty affect one's view of the Gospel?
6. Is there an urgency to the Gospel?
7. How does a lack of certainty affect the urgency of the Gospel?
8. What is the danger of hesitating when it comes to believing the Gospel?

5
Let's Make a Deal!

My style of deal-making is quite simple and straightforward. I aim very high, and then I just keep pushing and pushing and pushing to get what I'm after.
—Donald J. Trump

Let's Make a Deal is a television game show that first aired in the United States in 1963. Enormously successful, it soon expanded to many countries throughout the world. Monty Hall was the show's well-known and well-loved host for almost thirty years. Since 2009, *Let's Make a Deal* has aired weekday mornings in U.S. markets on CBS, and Wayne Brady is the show's current host. Although the format for the show varies somewhat in its different geographical markets, the basic idea involves contestants chosen from a studio audience being given the opportunity to make deals with the host.

The contestant starts with a prize of modest value, such as a new television or a couple hundred dollars in cash. The host then offers contestants the opportunity to trade what they have been given for another prize. There is a catch, however. The alternate prize is unknown. It is concealed behind one of three curtains. Depending on which curtain the contestant chooses, he or she could end up with a prize of far greater value, such as a new car or an exotic trip; or something of little or no value, such as a live goat or an old piece of furniture. When a contestant makes a deal that ends up netting him something absurd or worthless, he is said to have been "zonked."

The stakes at play in the game show *Let's Make a Deal* are all in good fun. If you have watched the show, you know it can be quite entertaining. In the business world, however, there is another level of deal-making that is far more serious. The stakes can be enormously high. Billionaire-turned-U.S. President Donald J. Trump outlines this brand of ruthless deal-making in his book *The Art of the Deal* (1987). In that book, Trump presents an eleven-step formula for financial success that includes principles such as "Think big," "Use leverage," "Don't be bullied," and "Maximize your options." He writes, "My style of deal-making is quite simple and straightforward. I aim very high, and then I just keep pushing and pushing and pushing to get what I'm after."

Trump credits his former pastor, Norman Vincent Peale, for influencing his outlook on life in general and his business success in particular. Peale was the pastor of New York City's Marble Collegiate Church for fifty-two years until his retirement in 1984. He was an influential Christian mystic who believed that our thoughts determine our destiny. He authored forty-six books, but is best known for his enormously popular book *The Power of Positive Thinking* (1952). The impact of this book on the world at large can hardly be overstated. It was on the New York Times Best Seller list for 186 consecutive weeks, including 48 weeks in the number-one position.

Peale's philosophy was that thoughts are causative: thoughts can change our lives, our health, and our destinies. His motto was, "If you believe it, you can have it, be it, or do it." Section titles in his book, such as "energy-producing thoughts," "spirit-lifters," and "faith attitudes," reveal his mystical ideology. Peale popularized sayings such as "Be all you can be" and "Think positive." He believed in reimagining your reality by picturing in your conscious mind a desired goal and focusing on that image until it becomes part of your unconscious mind, where it then releases powerful, untapped energy. Through this esoteric process, Peale taught, you can achieve success in any endeavor, including business deals.

Go Big or Go Home!

It is easy to see Peale's influence in Donald Trump's business model. The number-one principle in "Elements of the Deal" (chapter 2 in *The Art of the Deal*) is "Think big." He writes, "I like thinking big. I always have. To me it's very simple: If you're going to be thinking anyway, you might as well think big." He goes into every negotiation thinking he can win by "pushing and pushing and pushing," and most of the time he does, as evidenced by the financial empire he has built.

However, his success is not caused by some kind of outside force, ignited by his thoughts, that guarantees the desired results. Rather, it is more likely a consequence of Trump's relentless determination to get what he wants whatever the cost. His 2008 book, *Never Give Up*, further signals his win-at-all-costs outlook in life. At least six times, Trump's companies have filed for Chapter 11 bankruptcy protection, which means a company can remain in business while wiping away many of its debts—a corporate loophole that allows failure to be recast as success. "If at first you don't succeed, try, try again," and ignore the consequences of your poor decisions. Just keep "pushing and pushing and pushing."

This "think-it, believe-it" philosophy fosters an incipient pride that says, "I can accomplish whatever I set out to do no matter what it takes." Such an attitude, when taken to its extreme, can lead to an almost delusional sense of one's own abilities. Positive thinking really boils down to arrogant thinking: *I do not need anyone's help. I do not need breaks. I create my own breaks. If I work hard enough, negotiate ruthlessly enough, and never back down, I can achieve great success. I can do anything I set my mind to.* In other words, if you think it you can do it; therefore,

"Go big or go home." Norman Vincent Peale would be proud.

That Trump is a person given to grandiosity and narcissism is self-evident. It is pervasive in his writings and speeches, and it is especially noticeable now that he has taken office as the President of the United States. Consider the following quotes from Donald Trump taken from his own tweets, social media posts, interviews, and speeches:

"I'll be the greatest president that God ever created." (6/16/2015)

"Let me tell you, I'm a really smart guy." (10/30/2017)

"There's nobody bigger or better at the military than I am." (11/2015)

"I was successful, successful, successful. I was always the best athlete, people don't know that. But I was successful at everything I ever did." (1/14/2018)

"Nobody's ever been more successful than me." (1/1/2015)

"Nobody in the history of this country has ever known so much about infrastructure as Donald J. Trump." (7/2016)

"I will be the best by far in fighting terror. I'm the only one that was right from the beginning." (3/23/2016)

"I will be the greatest job-producing president in American history." (1/23/2016)

"Sorry losers and haters, but my I.Q. is one of the highest—and you all know it!" (5/8/2013)

"I was a good student. I understand things. I comprehend very well, better than I think almost anybody." (2/8/2017)

"I have proven to be far more correct about terrorism than anybody—and it's not even close." (3/22/2016)

"I'm honored to have the greatest temperament that anybody has." (11/3/2016)

"I have studied the Iran deal in great detail, greater by far than anyone else." (3/2016)

"I was always the best at what I did." (1/12/2018)

"Nobody knows the visa system better than me." (3/2016)

"Nobody knows more about foreign policy than I'll know on day one of my presidency." (10/2016)

"I can be more presidential than anybody but the great Abe Lincoln." (7/25/2017)

"No one reads the Bible more than me." (2/23/2016)

"I'm the world's greatest writer of 140-character sentences." (7/21/2014)

"I am the least racist person there is." (6/11/2016)

"I know more about ISIS than the generals do. Believe me." (11/12/2015)

"Nobody understands politicians like I do." (5/23/2013)

"I am the BEST builder, just look at what I've built." (5/13/2015)

"Nobody has more respect for women than Donald Trump!" (3/26/2016)

"No one has done more for people with disabilities than me." (2/9/2016)

"Nobody knows jobs like I do!" (1/8/2016)

"I am the only one who can fix this." (2/13/2016)

"Nobody but Donald Trump will save Israel." (4/27/2015)

"No politician in history has been treated more unfairly [than me]." (5/17/2017)

"I think I am, actually humble. I think I'm much more humble than you would understand." (7/17/2016)

Regardless of whether you like his style or not, there can be no doubt that Donald Trump has changed the face of the presidency forever. No president before him, Republican or Democrat, has ever spoken with such brazen self-aggrandizement. If "you are what you think," as Peale teaches, then Trump must really think he is invincible. This "go big or go home" attitude plays right into a worldview where life comes down to making the best deal. Tragically, many people

> **Tragically, many people will end up in hell someday because they think they can deal their way into heaven.**

will end up in hell someday because they think they can deal their way into heaven.

I've Got This!

Pride has always been the enemy of grace. Those who think they have no need of help will never humble themselves enough

> **No matter how determined you are, no matter how much you visualize heaven in your mind, no matter how good your negotiation skills may be, you cannot earn your place in heaven by striking a deal with God.**

to accept the very thing they need most. Grace and pride are mutually exclusive. Pride says, "I can do this on my own." Grace says, "I am helpless and hopeless; please save me." Seeking to solve your sin problem through self-help techniques, a relentless work ethic, or hard-nosed deal-making only digs your hole deeper. "Now to him who works, the wages are not counted as grace but as debt" (Romans 4:4). *We are not saved by works.* No matter how determined you are, no matter how much you visualize heaven in your mind, no matter how good your negotiation skills may be, you cannot earn your place in heaven by striking a deal with God.

If avoiding hell and entering heaven were a matter of negotiation, we would have something to brag about. In Trump-esque fashion, we could proclaim, "Nobody is better at making deals than me!" Or, "Look what I did! I am such a great deal-maker that I negotiated my way into heaven!" Trump himself seems to have adopted this "deal-making" approach to heaven: as he told a gathering of evangelical leaders in Orlando, Florida, on August 11, 2016, "For evangelicals, for the Christians, for the everybody, for everybody of religion, this will be, may be, the most important election that our country has ever had. And once I get in, I will do my thing that I do very well. And I figure it is probably, maybe the only way I'm going to get to heaven. So, I better do a good job."

Unfortunately for those of this ilk, the Bible is clear that eternal salvation cannot be achieved by our own efforts. "For by grace you have been saved through faith, and that not of yourselves; it is the gift of God, not of works, lest anyone should boast" (Ephesians 2:8–9).

An "I've got this!" kind of confidence might work well when you are stepping up to the plate in the bottom of the ninth inning or standing at the free throw line down by two points. However, eternity is not a game. Heaven cannot be obtained through willpower or tough-minded negotiation. We do not sit down

Heaven cannot be obtained through willpower or tough-minded negotiation.

at the bargaining table with God and say, "What will it take for me to get into heaven?" God has already told us what it will take: *perfection*. "For I say to you, that unless your righteousness exceeds the righteousness of the scribes and Pharisees, you will by no means enter the kingdom of heaven…. Therefore, you shall be perfect, just as your Father in heaven is perfect" (Matthew 5:20, 48).

Quid Pro Quo

As mentioned previously, entrance into heaven is not based upon a two-party contract. It is based upon a unilateral gift. There is no *quid pro quo* when it comes to entering heaven. Jesus often found Himself confronting this mentality during His earthly ministry. The self-righteous scribes and Pharisees thought they could earn a right standing before God through their own legalistic efforts. Jesus warned them, "You search the Scriptures, for in them you think you have eternal life; and these are they which testify of Me. But you are not willing to come to Me that you may have life" (John 5:39–40).

In other words, they thought that by keeping the Old Testament Law they would meet heaven's standard. Their side of the contract, they mistakenly assumed, amounted to obeying the Torah. Yet even their ancestral father Abraham was not justified by keeping the Law; "he believed in the Lord, and He accounted it to him for righteousness" (Genesis 15:6). We are "justified by faith in Christ and not by observing the law, because by observing the law no one will be justified" (Galatians 2:16, NIV). Jesus reminded them that the only way they could have eternal life was by coming to Him.

Elsewhere, Jesus told the scribes and Pharisees, "Not everyone who says to Me, 'Lord, Lord,' shall enter the kingdom of heaven, but he who does the will of My Father in heaven" (Matthew 7:21). What is the will of the Father? "And this is the

The perfect righteousness that heaven demands can only come by faith.

will of Him who sent Me, that everyone who sees the Son and

believes in Him may have everlasting life; and I will raise him up at the last day" (John 6:40). God wants everyone to believe in His Son and our Savior, Jesus Christ. "God is not willing that any should perish" (2 Peter 3:9). The perfect righteousness that heaven demands can only come by faith. It cannot be earned through good works; it must be received as a gift by faith. "Being justified by faith, we have peace with God through our Lord Jesus Christ" (Romans 5:1, KJV).

> For when we were still without strength, in due time Christ died for the ungodly. For scarcely for a righteous man will one die; yet perhaps for a good man someone would even dare to die. But God demonstrates His own love toward us, in that while we were still sinners, Christ died for us. Much more then, having now been justified by His blood, we shall be saved from wrath through Him. (Romans 5:6–9)

There is no *quid pro quo* with God. We have nothing to offer. "Nothing in our hands we bring, simply to the cross we cling." We are rescued from His wrath (i.e., eternity in hell) the moment we believe the Gospel. In that instantaneous moment when faith meets the Gospel, we "pass from death to life" and shall "never come into judgment" (John 5:24). In the words of Lewis Sperry Chafer, "To attempt to come unto God on the grounds of a public performance, even with great earnestness, is but to fail, and the misguided soul who makes that attempt, when his hope has proven false, is often the hardest to reach thereafter."

Failure to Perform

Let us say, for the sake of argument, that entrance into heaven was based upon a bilateral contract, and all we had to do was keep our end of the deal. The problem with this hypothetical scenario is that with any contract, if one party fails to keep the agreed-upon terms, the contract is null and void. It is a clause often called "failure to perform" or "breach of contract." If our eternal home in heaven was contingent upon our promise to "be good" or "serve God," as many people think it is, then the first time we sin or otherwise fail to faithfully serve God, all bets are off. Yet that is precisely what some well-respected Bible teachers of our day suggest. They teach that you cannot gain eternal life without first making a pledge of allegiance to Christ that involves forsaking all sin and following Him in unwavering obedience.

For example, John MacArthur believes that salvation comes not by simple faith alone, but by faith that includes "a redirection of the human will [and] a purposeful decision to forsake all unrighteousness and pursue righteousness instead." MacArthur and other Reformed scholars insist on the necessity of total surrender in order to be saved. In this view, you definitely must bring something to the bargaining table. According to this erroneous doctrine, at the end of the day no one will make it to heaven unless he has first produced some measure of visible good works in keeping with the contract he made with God. John Piper, for example, writes, "There is no doubt that Jesus saw some measure of real, lived-out obedience to the will of God as necessary for final salvation."

In a similar vein, MacArthur believes, "There is an inseparable relationship between obedience and faith—almost like two sides of a coin. It is impossible to detach one from the other." He adds, "People have a right to be suspicious of one who says he believes in Jesus but fails to live up to that claim." Regarding good works, James Montgomery Boice insists, "If we are not doing them, this is also a sign that we are not genuinely converted." In other words, we failed to perform on the contract, so we have no assurance of heaven. (Moreover, the fact that no human can actually fulfill this sort of pledge also means that such a "contract" is null and void from the beginning.) These scholars who insist on good works as a determinative factor on whether or not a person goes to heaven claim to believe in salvation by faith alone in Christ alone. However, they maintain that works are the inevitable and required result of faith.

MacArthur puts it this way, "Where there are no works, we must assume no faith exists either." Similarly, R. C. Sproul writes, "True faith shows itself in good deeds." Such thinking is contrary to the unambiguous testimony of Scripture that describes the requirement for receiving the free gift of eternal life only in terms of faith, not faith that promises obedience or good works. Scholars like MacArthur, Piper, Sproul, and Boice contend that you cannot get something as valuable as eternal life merely by believing in Jesus Christ as the Son of God who died and rose again for your sins. That would be too easy, and, according to MacArthur, it should be "hard to believe."

Yet Jesus made it clear that faith is not complex at all. It is so simple even a child can believe the Gospel. Jesus said, "Let the little children come to Me, and do not forbid them; for of such is the kingdom of God. Assuredly, I say to you, whoever does not receive the kingdom of God as a little child will by no means enter it" (Mark 10:14–15). The Bible tell us, "Then Jesus called a little child to Him, set him in the midst of them, and said, 'Assuredly, I say to you, unless you are converted and become as little children, you will by no means enter the kingdom of heaven. Therefore whoever humbles himself as this little child is the greatest in the kingdom of heaven'" (Matthew 18:2–4).

Children understand simple faith. They know what it means to trust in someone. Adults have made faith far more complicated than it really is. As Charles Swindoll writes, "Salvation is a free gift. You simply lay hold of what Christ has provided. Period. And yet the heretical doctrine of works goes on all around the world and always will. It is effective because the pride of men and women is so strong. We simply have to do something in order to feel right about it. It just doesn't make good humanistic sense to get something valuable for nothing." Consequently, many people think they have to negotiate with God by making promises and pledges to Him in order to earn their way to heaven. However, the standard is perfect righteousness, which can only be received as a gift by faith.

> The fact that the unregenerate are blinded by Satan in regard to the true Gospel of grace is the explanation of the age-long plea of the moralist: "If I do the best I can, God must be satisfied with that, else He is unreasonable." Granting that anyone has ever done his best, it would still be most imperfect as compared with the infinite holiness of God. God cannot, under any conditions, call that perfect which is imperfect, and He is far from unreasonable in demanding a perfect righteousness, impossible to man, while He stands ready to provide as a gift all that His holiness requires. This is exactly the offer of the Gospel (Lewis Sperry Chafer).

There are no moral demands that an unsaved person can meet in an effort to negotiate with God and get into heaven. God's salvation is not a matter of deal-making. It is a free gift received only by faith.

Don't Get Zonked!

Someday there will be millions of people facing judgment before the Great White Throne who expect to receive eternal life based upon their understanding of a contract they thought they made with God. They will come armed with documentation to "prove" that they did their part, that they kept their end of the deal. Indeed, their

> **There are no moral demands that an unsaved person can meet in an effort to negotiate with God and get into heaven.**

judgment will be based upon a collection of books in which all of their good deeds will be recorded. Tragically, however, these books will not be enough. The Bible describes the scene vividly:

> And I saw the dead, small and great, standing before God, and books were opened. And another book was opened, which is the Book of Life. And the dead were judged according to their works, by the things which were written in the books. The sea gave up the dead who were in it, and Death and Hades delivered up the dead who were in them. And they were judged, each one according to his works. Then Death and Hades were cast into the lake of fire. This is the second death. And anyone not found written in the Book of Life was cast into the lake of fire. (Revelation 20:12–15)

In the end, there is only one book that matters: *The Book of Life*. In it are recorded the names of everyone who has accepted the free gift of eternal life by faith alone in Christ alone. Books of works, no matter how voluminous, can never contain enough good deeds to open the doors of heaven. Making a bad deal on a game show is one thing; gambling with your

> **Making a bad deal on a game show is one thing; gambling with your eternity is another.**

eternity is another. Some people may end up in hell one day because they thought they could negotiate their way into a right standing before a holy God. They thought that they could escape hell by striking a deal with the Creator and keeping their end of the bargain. However, the Bible is clear that entrance into heaven is not the result of some kind of bilateral contract with God. It is a free gift received only by faith alone in Christ alone.

Those who make the wrong choice on *Let's Make a Deal* might hear Wayne Brady say, "You've been zonked!" The loser in a high-dollar financial negotiation might hear, "You've been had!" Unfortunately, those who think they can wheel and deal their way into heaven based upon their performance on earth will hear a far more somber declaration from Jesus Christ: "Depart from Me into the everlasting fire" (Matthew 25:41).

For Further Consideration

1. Is our salvation based upon a bilateral contract between us and God, or is it based upon a unilateral gift from God?

2. What are some reasons that many people think they can negotiate with God and wheel and deal their way into heaven?

3. Describe how pride underlies the "Let's make a deal!" philosophy of getting into heaven.

4. Why is simple faith alone in Christ alone so difficult for some people to understand?

5. What are some common false teachings that have clouded the issue of faith and caused it to be redefined as a pledge, promise, or commitment?

6. Assuming for the sake of argument that salvation could in fact be obtained by negotiating a two-way contract with God, what would be the problem?

7. Of what value are our good works when it comes to getting into heaven?

6
The G.O.A.T.

As long as you are proud you cannot know God. A proud man is always looking down on things and people: and, of course, as long as you are looking down you cannot see something that is above you.
—C. S. Lewis, *Mere Christianity*

Muhammad Ali, arguably the greatest boxer of all time, was known for his braggadocious style. As a young boy, I was a fan of his, not only because I grew up watching his storied bouts on television with my father, but also because I had a serendipitous face-to-face encounter with him when I was about eleven years old. My family lived in western Connecticut at the time, and my father worked in New York City. Family shopping trips and sightseeing trips to Manhattan were a common occurrence for us. On one of those trips we happened to run into Ali and his entourage on the sidewalk outside an upscale clothing store. My mother hastily grabbed a pen and scrap of paper from her purse, and I secured a cherished autograph.

Whether Ali was actually the G.O.A.T., "greatest of all time," is open for debate, but one thing is certain: he thought he was the greatest! "I'm not the greatest; I'm the double greatest. Not only do I knock 'em out; I pick the round," he once boasted. He declared, "It's hard to be humble when you're as great as I am," and "It's not bragging if you can back it up." He would taunt and threaten his opponents in the days leading up to a big fight with statements like, "If you even dream of beating me you'd better wake up and apologize." He said of one famous nemesis, "I've seen George Foreman shadowboxing, and the shadow won."

One of his most famous lines was, "I float like a butterfly, sting like a bee. The hands can't hit what the eyes can't see." My personal favorite Ali quote is, "I'm so fast that last night I turned off the light switch in my hotel room and I was in bed before the room was dark." One might argue that such brazen pride sits well on an athletic superstar; it goes with the territory. However, it is not so attractive coming from your average person. In fact, it can be rather annoying. More than that, pride can be detrimental. The Bible cautions, "Pride goes before destruction, and a haughty spirit before a fall" (Proverbs 16:18).

Narcissism Epidemic

By all accounts, our current culture is facing what many experts are calling a "narcissism epidemic." The cover of *Time* magazine called it the "Me, Me, Me Generation." *Newsweek* had a feature piece, "Narcissism on the Rise in America." Millennials have taken the brunt of the criticism, but it would seem the problem is broader than that. Best-selling books such as *Unmasking Narcissism* (Ettensohn and Simon, 2016), *Rethinking Narcissism* (Malkin, 2015), and *The Narcissist Next Door* (Kluger, 2015) make a compelling case that we are more self-absorbed today than at any other time in human history. The Christian community is by no means immune, as one author suggests in his book, *When Narcissism Comes to Church* (DeGroat, 2020).

The term *narcissist* comes from Greek mythology. As the story goes, Narcissus was a very handsome fellow who exhibited profound indifference and disregard toward others. The gods punished him by causing him to fall in love with his own image. One day, while adoring himself in the mirror, he was so taken by his own beauty that he was unable to pull himself away, and he eventually wasted away and died. The mental picture of this mythological episode calls to mind the millions of selfies that are pervasive on Facebook and other social media outlets these days. Indeed, many researchers have suggested that the role of social media in our culture may be having a direct impact on the meteoric rise of narcissism. It is difficult for young people in today's culture to remember, as Franklin D. Roosevelt put it, "you are just an extra in everybody else's play."

Of course, prideful self-absorption is nothing new. Pride was the original sin when the angel Lucifer said in his heart, "I will ascend into heaven; I will exalt my throne above the stars of God" (Isaiah 14:13). Like Narcissus, the devil's heart "was lifted up because of [his] beauty," so God "cast [him] to the ground" (Ezekiel 28:17). As early as one thousand years before Christ, pride occupied the number-one spot on the list of so-called seven deadly sins in the Bible (Proverbs 6:17), and many other ancient texts similarly warn about the dangers of an unchecked ego. However, there seems to be something different about the upsurge of narcissism in our current culture.

Today, arrogance is celebrated, encouraged, and rewarded. In a 2019 article for the online magazine Trending US, one business expert states flatly, "Being arrogant is good." She goes on to identify several reasons why arrogance will help you get ahead in the business world. Today's young professionals are in-your-face about their pride. "Just because I am arrogant doesn't mean I am not right!" they say, ratcheting up the rhetoric. Even secular social scientists are concerned. "It's one thing to see that there is a growing number of narcissists in America today," observes one sociologist, "but the real concern is not the individual narcissists among us, but when our society embraces narcissism as the norm." A journalist from *The Guardian* asks, "From attention-seeking celebrities to digital oversharing and the boom in cosmetic surgery, narcissistic behavior is all around us. How worried should we be about our growing self-obsession?" Albert

> **Today, arrogance is celebrated, encouraged, and rewarded.**

Einstein was a pretty smart man and he thought we should be very worried. He famously warned, "The only thing more dangerous than ignorance is arrogance."

I am no Einstein, but I do know that the Bible agrees. When it comes to the impact of narcissistic thinking on one's view of sin, salvation, and eternity, we should be especially concerned. Scripture warns us that "the pride of life" (1 John 2:16) is part of the world's system, a world run by the "god of this age," Satan, who is blinding human hearts to the Gospel (2 Corinthians 4:4). Many people will end up in hell some day because their own pride would not allow them to understand and believe the Gospel message. Pride blinds people to their sinful state; before you can be found you must realize you are lost.

> **Pride blinds people to their sinful state.**

Lost and Found

Throughout Jesus' earthly ministry He spent time with the meek and downtrodden, those who were social outcasts. The self-righteous scribes, Pharisees, and Sadducees never could understand why He did so. They often confronted Him for associating with dirty rotten sinners, such as harlots and lepers. They asked Him one time, "Why do You eat and drink with tax collectors and sinners?" (Luke 5:30). Jesus responded, "Those who are well have no need of a physician, but those who are sick. I have not come to call the righteous, but sinners, to repentance" (Luke 5:31–32). In other words, Jesus focused on those whose life circumstance made them humble, those who knew they needed help and were willing to change their minds (repent) about Jesus. By contrast, those who were perfectly righteous, or thought they were, had no interest in what Jesus was offering.

On another occasion, Jesus gave a longer answer when the self-righteous Pharisees complained about the company He was keeping. The Bible says, "Then all the tax collectors and the sinners drew near to Him to hear Him. And the Pharisees and scribes complained, saying, 'This Man receives sinners and eats with them.' So He spoke this parable to them" (Luke 15:1–3). What follows in Luke's account is an extended lesson from the Lord Himself in the form of three parables—and this lesson is very important.

The first parable deals with a lost sheep. Jesus asks, "What man of you, having a hundred sheep, if he loses one of them, does not leave the ninety-nine in the wilderness, and go after the one which is lost until he finds it?" (Luke 15:4). Note that the focus is on the one sheep that has a problem, not the ninety-nine that are just fine as they are. Any shepherd worth his salt is going to focus his time and energy on the wandering sheep, not the herd that is safe and sound, grazing in the field. Moreover, when a lost sheep is found it is cause for great joy. Jesus leaves no doubt about the point He is making. He explicitly states, "I say to you that likewise there will be more joy in heaven over one sinner who repents than over ninety-nine just persons who need no repentance" (Luke 15:7).

This parable about the lost sheep and the two parables that follow it deal with matters of eternal significance. Jesus' use of the word "just" to describe those who need no repentance is important. The Greek word translated "just" (*dikaios*) is the same word translated elsewhere as "righteous." For instance, in Romans 3:10 the same word is used when the Bible declares, "There is none *righteous*, no, not one." The Pharisees *thought* they were righteous, and they were unwilling to change their minds (repent). They certainly considered themselves more righteous than anyone else, and righteous enough to get into heaven. However, Jesus had previously stated, "I say to you, that unless your righteousness exceeds the righteousness of the scribes and Pharisees, you will by no means enter the kingdom of heaven" (Matthew 5:20). Whatever level of righteousness they had attained; it was not enough.

Jesus refers to "just persons" in this parable in the sense of "those who think they are righteous," not those who actually were. The only way to obtain the righteousness that heaven demands is to humble yourself, recognize your need, and accept Christ's righteousness by faith. "Through one Man's righteous act the free gift came to all men, resulting in justification of life" (Romans 5:18). "For [God] made Him who knew no sin to be sin for us, that we might become the righteousness of God in Him" (2 Corinthians 5:21). When you place your faith in Jesus Christ as the only One who can save you, you are declared perfectly righteous in Christ. "Having been justified by faith, we have peace with God through our Lord Jesus Christ" (Romans 5:1).

> The only way to obtain the righteousness that heaven demands is to humble yourself, recognize your need, and accept Christ's righteousness by faith.

Being "justified" means that Christ's perfect righteousness has been imputed to you—charged to your account. It means you are a new creation in Christ, and His blood covers your sins once and for all. "If anyone is in Christ, he is a new creation" (2 Corinthians 5:17). This does not mean that you will never sin again. It means that your sin can never condemn you to hell. The moment you believe the Gospel, you receive the Holy Spirit as a "deposit guaranteeing your inheritance" in heaven (Ephesians 1:14, NIV). The Holy Spirit leads, guides, and directs believers who yield to Him. He does not force Christians to obey, however, and Christians who choose *not* to yield to the

Holy Spirit will still sin. Nevertheless, their identity in Christ can never change. Sin in the life of a believer grieves the Holy Spirit and breaks our fellowship with God, but it can never cause Him to disown one of His children; and everyone who believes the Gospel becomes a "child of God" at the moment of faith (John 1:12).

There is a difference between being part of the family of God and being in fellowship with God. We become part of the family of God, "adopted as sons" (Galatians 4:5), the moment we believe in Jesus Christ and Him alone for salvation. Our spiritual DNA is once and for all identified with Christ. Just as our physical DNA will always connect us to our earthly parents, our spiritual DNA will always connect us to our heavenly Father. Jesus said, "And I give them eternal life, and they shall never perish; neither shall anyone snatch them out of My hand. My Father, who has given them to Me, is greater than all; and no one is able to snatch them out of My Father's hand" (John 10:28–29).

Fellowship within the family of God is another matter. Just as physical relatives might find their relationship strained at times — a mother with a daughter, a brother with a sister — yet remain family members, likewise sin in the life of a believer breaks fellowship with God. It grieves the Holy Spirit when believers sin, and it interrupts the lines of communication we have with God. "The Lord is far from the wicked, but He hears the prayer of the righteous" (Proverbs 15:29). "If I regard iniquity in my heart, the Lord will not hear" (Psalm 66:18). Jesus told His disciples, "abide in Me." The word "abide" in Greek (*meno*) means to remain in close fellowship. "For without Me," Jesus continued, "you can do nothing" (John 15:4–5). In other words, the closer we stay to the Lord through godly living, prayer, Bible study, worship, and so on, the better life will be. The family bond we have in Christ can never be broken, although fellowship can be broken. Thankfully, the sweetness of fellowship with our Lord can always be restored simply by coming to Him in brokenness and confession (1 John 1:9).

It is likely that this first parable about a lost sheep would have called to remembrance in the minds of the Pharisees the great prophet Isaiah's words, "All we like sheep have gone astray; we have turned, every one, to his own way; and the Lord has laid on Him the iniquity of us all" (Isaiah 53:6). The Pharisees were well acquainted with the prophet Isaiah's words. What they missed was that the lost sheep did not scratch and claw his way back into the fold through his own efforts. A lost sheep has nothing to boast about. He needs his shepherd to rescue him. Jesus Christ, our Shepherd, paid our sin debt when He died on the cross and rose again. Jesus said, "I am the good shepherd. The good shepherd gives His life for the sheep" (John 10:11). Elsewhere He said, "The Son of Man has come to seek and to save that which was lost" (Luke 19:10).

Without Jesus, people wander aimlessly trying to solve their own sin problem. Only through Jesus, the Savior of the world, can anyone have life. The Bible tells us that "the Father has sent the Son as Savior of the world" (1 John 4:14). "In this the love of God was manifested toward us, that God has sent His only begotten Son into the world, that we might live through Him. In this is love, not that we loved God, but that He loved us and

> **Without Jesus, people wander aimlessly trying to solve their own sin problem.**

sent His Son to be the propitiation for our sins" (1 John 4:9–10). "This is a faithful saying and worthy of all acceptance, that Christ Jesus came into the world to save sinners" (1 Timothy 1:15).

Jesus tells a second parable in response to the Pharisees' criticism of His social interactions. He asks, "What woman, having ten silver coins, if she loses one coin, does not light a lamp, sweep the house, and search carefully until she finds it?" (Luke 15:8). Although His metaphor shifts from one hundred sheep to ten coins, His point is the same. It is the lost coin that matters; it is the lost soul that Jesus cares most about. The Pharisees undoubtedly would have identified with the actions of the woman and the shepherd in prioritizing what was lost. Who wouldn't do the same? Obviously anyone would try to find a lost coin and rescue a lost sheep.

However, the essence of what Jesus was saying was still unclear to them. They did not catch that He was equating the items of priority in the parable—the lost coin and sheep—with His prioritizing of the sinners with whom He was spending His time. To drive the point home, Jesus tells one final parable that is much longer, with much greater detail, than the first two. This time it is not one hundred sheep or ten coins that serve as the focus of His story, but only two brothers; and both of them are Jews. Which brother would the Pharisees identify with?

An Unlikely Hero

The parable of the lost son, commonly known as the "prodigal son," is well known to most people. Two brothers are raised by a devout Jewish father who loved them both equally. The younger son demands his inheritance, leaves home, violates all manner of Jewish laws, squanders all his money, and finds himself penniless and homeless. The Pharisees, listening to Jesus unpack this story, would have been repulsed by the actions of the rebellious younger brother. In His typical fashion, however, Jesus' story has a plot twist where the antagonist in the tale becomes the hero. Take a look at the first part of the story.

> A certain man had two sons. And the younger of them said to his father, "Father, give me the portion of goods that falls to me." So he divided to them his livelihood. And not

many days after, the younger son gathered all together, journeyed to a far country, and there wasted his possessions with prodigal living. But when he had spent all, there arose a severe famine in that land, and he began to be in want. Then he went and joined himself to a citizen of that country, and he sent him into his fields to feed swine. And he would gladly have filled his stomach with the pods that the swine ate, and no one gave him anything. (Luke 15:11–16)

No self-respecting Jew would have conducted himself the way the prodigal son did. You can almost see the Pharisees wrinkling their noses and raising their eyebrows as Jesus describes his selfish, sinful behavior. When the prodigal ends up in a pigpen, lonely and hungry, the Pharisees no doubt thought he got what he deserved. After all, their philosophy was that only those who keep every jot and tittle of the Law deserve blessing; only the (self) righteous deserve heaven. As the story continues, their disdain for the younger brother only grows.

But when he came to himself, he said, "How many of my father's hired servants have bread enough and to spare, and I perish with hunger! I will arise and go to my father, and will say to him, 'Father, I have sinned against heaven and before you, and I am no longer worthy to be called your son. Make me like one of your hired servants.'" (Luke 15:17–19)

When the rebellious son decides to come crawling back home, the Pharisees were probably on the edge of their seats waiting to see what would happen. Would the father reject him? Turn him away? Beat him? Worse? What would this filthy, dirty, rotten, sinner get? "Throw the book at him," they shouted in their minds. What the Pharisees failed to notice, though, was one small phrase that the prodigal recited as he practiced the conversation he planned to have with his father. "I am no longer worthy," he would tell his father. There it is. That simple statement is the point of all three parables. Only those who acknowledge their unworthiness, and in simple humility come to the One who can rescue them, will find forgiveness. Those who think they are "just," and have no need of salvation, are the ones with the real problem. Imagine the Pharisees' surprise with the plot twist that comes next.

> **Only those who acknowledge their unworthiness, and in simple humility come to the One who can rescue them, will find forgiveness.**

And he arose and came to his father. But when he was still a great way off, his father saw him and had compassion, and ran and fell on his neck and kissed him. And the son said to him, "Father, I have sinned against heaven and in your sight, and am no longer worthy to be called your son." But the father said to his servants, "Bring out the best robe and put it on him, and put a ring on his hand and sandals on his feet. And bring the fatted calf here and kill it, and let us eat and be merry; for this my son was dead and is alive again; he was lost and is found." And they began to be merry. (Luke 15:20–24)

No scolding. No lecture. No rejection. No slammed doors or beatings. Just a warm, compassionate embrace. The prodigal found love—*unconditional* love. Just as there was rejoicing over the rescued sheep and the recovered coin in the first two parables, there was joy in this one as well: joy over the son who "was lost and is found." Jesus'

> **The doors of heaven are open, not to those who have it all together, but to those who recognize that they don't.**

point could not be clearer. Throughout His ministry He repeatedly offered forgiveness and eternal life to all who would simply come to Him. "Come to Me, all you who labor and are heavy laden, and I will give you rest," He said (Matthew 11:28). "I am the bread of life. He who comes to Me shall never hunger, and he who believes in Me shall never thirst" (John 6:35). The doors of heaven are open, not to those who have it all together, but to those who recognize that they don't. This is the part the prideful Pharisees missed, as do many people today.

The story does not end there, however. There is one more surprise. In an effort to drive home His point, Jesus brings the older son into the plotline of His parable. How would the older son respond to his father's gracious and merciful treatment of his younger brother? The older son had done nothing wrong; he had obeyed the rules, kept the Law, and honored his father. Sound familiar? Jesus wanted the Pharisees to identify with the older son, and the reaction of the older son in the parable served as an indictment of the Pharisees' outlook toward sinners and tax collectors.

> Now his older son was in the field. And as he came and drew near to the house, he heard music and dancing. So he called one of the servants and asked what these things meant. And he said to him, "Your brother has come, and because he has received him safe and sound, your father has killed the fatted calf." But he was angry and would not go in. Therefore his father came out and pleaded with him. So he answered and said to his father, "Lo, these many years I have been serving you; I never transgressed your commandment at any time; and yet you never gave me a young goat, that I might make merry with my friends. But as soon as this son of yours came, who has devoured your livelihood with harlots, you killed the fatted calf for him." And he said to him, "Son, you are always with me, and all that I have is yours. It was right that we should make merry

and be glad, for your brother was dead and is alive again, and was lost and is found." (Luke 15:25–32)

The older brother sought to justify himself. "Look what I've done," he protested. "I have never transgressed your commandment at any time," he declared, in a statement reminiscent of the rich young ruler's attitude. Essentially he was comparing himself to his younger brother and claiming to be better. "Since I am better," he reasoned, "I deserve the fatted calf and fancy robe." Such was the attitude of the Pharisees. It was all about comparison. They looked down their noses at the "sinners and tax collectors." They needed to look in the mirror. Only those who humble themselves, admit their unworthiness, and come empty-handed to Jesus can receive the free gift of eternal life and forgiveness of sins.

Do not miss the father's response to the older brother. "Son, you are always with me, and all that I have is yours." This is the message Jesus had for the nation of Israel and its self-righteous leaders. "I am here for you. All I have is yours," He said. Yet, "He came to His own, and His own did not receive Him" (John 1:11). They thought they were righteous enough because they were better than everyone else. If they would only humble themselves, change their minds, and come to Christ, they could be saved. Sadly, they overlooked Jesus' plain statement in His first major sermon—the Sermon on the Mount—that entrance into heaven requires righteousness greater than anything the Pharisees could muster up. The righteousness that heaven demands is perfect righteousness (Matthew 5:17, 20), and that only comes through a relationship with Christ.

> Only those who humble themselves, admit their unworthiness, and come empty-handed to Jesus can receive the free gift of eternal life and forgiveness of sins.

In that same sermon, Jesus had pointed out that while these arrogant Jewish leaders are prating and boasting about how they have never committed any of the "big sins" such as murder or adultery, in reality their attitudes of hatred and lust have broken these very laws. Jesus pointedly said to them, "You have heard that it was said to those of old, 'You shall not murder, and whoever murders will be in danger of the judgment.' But I say to you that whoever is angry with his brother without a cause shall be in danger of the judgment" (Matthew 5:21–22). And again, "You have heard that it was said to those of old, 'You shall not commit adultery.' But I say to you that whoever looks at a woman to lust for her has already committed adultery with her in his heart" (Matthew 5:27–28). In other words, everyone is a sinner because it is what's in your heart that matters, not your outward behavior. "The heart is deceitful above all things, and desperately wicked; who can know it?" (Jeremiah 17:9).

Perhaps most offensive was the way these self-righteous Jews looked down their noses at those from the lower tiers of the Jewish social strata. They judged others for their more visible "big sins," yet failed to recognize that their own attitudes were just as offensive to God. Jesus reminded them to be careful about pointing out the speck in their neighbor's eye, when in reality there was a great big plank protruding from their own eye (Matthew 7:1–5).

Pride blinds people to their sinful state; before you can be found you must realize you are lost.

Pride blinds people to their sinful state; before you can be found you must realize you are lost.

Grading on a Curve

As we saw with the older brother in the parable of the lost son, an attitude of pride leads to a comparison mentality: "I'm better than…," "I am more deserving than…," and so on. However, when it comes to the plan of salvation, the only point of comparison that matters is Jesus. Are you perfect? If not, you need Him to give you His righteousness. Only Jesus has the right to forgive sin and give life. Jesus said, "The Son gives life to whom He will" (John 5:21). God does not grade on a curve.

The standard for entering heaven is not like the standard for entering college. It is not about being in the ninetieth percentile on your SAT scores. It is not about graduating in the top ten percent of your class. Entering heaven is not based upon how well you have done compared to others. This Pharisaical view is alive and well today among those who like to keep score. They mistakenly assume that the standard for entering heaven is "most people." As long as they are "better than most people," or "not as bad as the worst," they think, "I will get into heaven." The problem is that *all people are sinners*; so comparing yourself to everyone else is like asking which fish in the ocean is the wettest. There is no evaluation by comparison when it comes to getting into heaven.

> **The problem is that *all people are sinners*, so comparing yourself to everyone else is like asking which fish in the ocean is the wettest.**

I will close this chapter with one more Muhammad Ali anecdote. As the story goes, Ali was sitting on a plane about to take off from LaGuardia Airport. When a flight attendant asked him to buckle his seatbelt, Ali grumbled, "Superman don't need no seatbelt." The quick-thinking flight attendant responded, "Superman don't need no plane, either. Buckle up!" Plane crashes are no respecter of person, and neither is God. You might be good. You might be great. Perhaps you are greater than most. Or, better yet, maybe even the greatest of all time. It does not matter. God does not grade on a curve. Some people who think they are the "G.O.A.T." may find themselves among many goats in hell for all eternity (Matthew 25:31–46).

For Further Consideration

1. Why is narcissism an enemy of the Gospel?

2. How does pride blind people to their need for a Savior?

3. Who do you identify with more in the parable of the prodigal son, the older brother or the younger brother? Why?

4. How good do you have to be to get into heaven?

5. What is the standard for entrance into heaven?

6. What do we mean when we say, "God does not grade on a curve"?

7. How does humility relate to faith?

8. How does pride relate to a performance mentality?

7

Mending a Broken Heart

How can you mend this broken man? How can a loser ever win? Please help me mend my broken heart and let me live again. —Barry Gibb

When my eldest daughter was about three years old, she used to respond to being scolded by saying, with all of the attendant emotional sobs and tears, "Daddy, you broke my heart!" I can still hear her saying it today. Like most toddlers, she did not like being told, "No!" Her outburst was mostly for dramatic effect. "You broke my heart" was her way of saying that I had hurt her feelings and she was unhappy. She may even have been trying to get me to change my decision. I probably did not help the situation by responding, "Oh, your heart is broken? Bring me my hammer and I'll see if I can fix it!"

Some broken hearts go much deeper than a young child's theatrics. Have you ever been brokenhearted? Have you ever experienced the deep inner pain that makes you feel like your heart has been ripped from your chest? Heartache so tangible, that it really, truly hurts—physically? Maybe it was caused by the end of a relationship, or perhaps it was the loss of a loved one. Maybe a friend said something or did something that hurt you deeply. We have all been there. Our hearts are tender, fragile organs, both physically and emotionally. Traditionally, the heart represents the seat of our thoughts, feelings, and emotions; and in fact the heart is a primary partner of the brain in creating and processing all of these. The heart is where we wrestle with spiritual issues and struggle against sin. The heart is intimately involved when we contemplate life and form ideas that eventually become actions. When we are faced with a crisis, tragedy, or other painful stimulus, our hearts can be broken.

How do we respond to sorrow? Or, as Barry and Robin Gibb put it, "How can you mend a broken heart?" This famous Bee Gees song expresses the emotion of heartache well:

I can think of younger days when living for my life
Was everything a man could want to do.
I could never see tomorrow, but I was never told about the sorrow.
And how can you mend a broken heart?
How can you stop the rain from falling down?
How can you stop the sun from shining?
What makes the world go round?
How can you mend this broken man?
How can a loser ever win?
Please help me mend my broken heart and let me live again.

I can still feel the breeze that rustles through the trees
And misty memories of days gone by
We could never see tomorrow, no one said a word about the sorrow.

What a powerful song. Did you notice that it asks heart-wrenching questions, but does not provide any answers? Somewhere, someone suggested that time heals all wounds. Perhaps that is true, yet surely there is something more palatable to the aching soul than simply waiting. "Hang in there. It will get better with time," sounds so empty and useless when your heart is truly weighted down with pain and sorrow. A better solution is found by transcending the temporal arena of time and space and coming at the problem from a spiritual perspective. What does the Bible say?

Centuries ago, King David faced a heartbreaking time. He was fleeing from Saul, alone and separated from his dear friend Jonathan, in serious danger. In that context he wrote, "The righteous cry out, and the Lord hears, and delivers them out of all their troubles. The Lord is near to those who have a broken heart and saves such as have a contrite spirit" (Psalm 34:17–18). The word *broken* here comes from a Hebrew root word, *shabar*, that means "to destroy, shatter, or crush violently." The word *contrite* is equally strong. It comes from a Hebrew root word, *dakka*, that means "to crush something until it becomes dust or powder." In other words, when David speaks of a "broken heart" and "contrite spirit," he is speaking of intense hurt and pain.

In Psalm 69 David puts it this way: "Reproach has broken my heart, and I am full of heaviness; I looked for someone to take pity, but there was none; and for comforters, but I found none" (Psalm 69:20). About four hundred years after David, Jeremiah the prophet also spoke of a broken heart. He is so heartbroken that he cannot walk. It is as if he is drunk. "My heart within me is broken because of the prophets; all my bones shake. I am like a drunken man, and like a man whom wine has overcome" (Jeremiah 23:9).

An anonymous psalmist uses a similar analogy. Referring to brokenhearted Israelites he says, "Their soul melts because of trouble. They reel to and fro, and stagger like a drunken man, and are at their wits' end" (Psalm 107:26–27). The phrase "at their wits' end" in Hebrew is literally "all their wisdom is swallowed up." In other words, when our heart is broken, when our soul is melting, we cannot explain it or understand it or even think about it. We just stagger around like a drunkard in a daze. For many, this brokenhearted condition becomes a lifetime ailment. The longer they hurt, the more out of reach hope seems. Tragically, because of deep heartache, many people refuse to believe the Gospel and end up in hell.

The Blame Game

Those who have experienced intense sorrow often become bitter and look for someone or something to blame. At first they may blame their circumstances, or themselves, or maybe a friend, relative, or acquaintance. Inevitably, though, their thoughts turn to God. "How could God allow this to happen?" they wonder. This makes it even harder to trust Him when it comes to their eternal destiny. "Why should I trust the One who has caused me so much hurt and pain?" they reason. This type of thinking is common among those who feel hopeless. Ironically, they shut out the very One who can actually bring comfort and solve their problem. At times, even spiritual giants like King David expressed bitterness toward God. At one point, he cried out, "How long, O Lord? Will You forget me forever? How long will You hide Your face from me? How long shall I take counsel in my soul, having sorrow in my heart daily? How long will my enemy be exalted over me?" (Psalm 13:1–2).

However, David did not allow that viewpoint to linger forever. Eventually, he acknowledged that God is not the source of his pain, but rather the cure for it. "But I have trusted in Your mercy; my heart shall rejoice in Your salvation" (Psalm 13:5). The Hebrew word translated "salvation" here, *yeshuah*, simply means deliverance or rescue. David knew that God could and would rescue him in the midst of his heartache. Returning to David's words in Psalm 34, we see that in his despair he sought refuge in the Lord. He believed that "The Lord is near to those who have a broken heart and saves such as have a contrite spirit" (Psalm 34:18). He expected the Lord to rescue ("save") him. This verse is comforting, but it leaves me

> Those who have experienced intense sorrow often become bitter and look for someone or something to blame.

wanting more. You say the Lord is near when my heart aches. That's good, but what does it do for me? I understand that He rescues me from a broken heart, but tell me more: *How* does He do that? Why can't I feel Him taking my heart in His hand, soothing it, calming it, and making it feel better? Why does it still hurt?

Psalm 34:18 is part of a larger psalm that, taken as a whole, gives us more than a sound bite; it gives us a roadmap for mending a broken heart. Unlike the Bee Gees' famous song, this psalm is not just a series of depressing, unanswered questions. It has answers. Let's walk through it together and take it one step at a time. To those who refuse to believe the Gospel because their hearts are broken and the outlook seems dim, I say: Give God a chance. Let Him prove to you why He is the answer, not the problem.

You are not alone

The first thing you need to remember when your heart is broken is that you are not alone. When you are suffering from a broken heart, the tendency is to feel alone and abandoned. The only thing worse than being brokenhearted is being broken-hearted and alone. Loneliness and brokenheartedness are twin evils. One is more than anyone should ever have to face. Both

> **The first thing you need to remember when your heart is broken is that you are not alone.**

at once? Unbearable! David reminds us, "The Lord is near" (Psalm 34:18). This is the same David who declared in the famous twenty-third Psalm, "Yea, though I walk through the valley of the shadow of death, I will fear no evil; for You are with me; Your rod and Your staff, they comfort me" (Psalm 23:4).

David understood the heartaches of life from two distinct perspectives. As a shepherd, he had experienced fear, danger, darkness, and predatory enemies while protecting his flock. As the king of God's chosen nation, Israel, he had also experienced fear, danger, and threats from enemy nations. In Psalm 23 he draws from both experiences to gain comfort in times of trouble. Like a shepherd, God has both a rod and a staff. He directs our steps and rescues us from precarious situations. Like a shepherd who leads his flock to green pastures and still waters, God also provides for our needs. Moreover, like a victorious king, God also prepares a victory feast for us and makes our enemies watch as we celebrate. "You prepare a table before me in the presence of my enemies; You anoint my head with oil; my cup runs over" (Psalm 23:5).

It was common in the ancient Near East for a king to host a banquet celebrating his victory in war against a rival nation. This is what David is referring to at the end of Psalm 23. Instead of his enemies relentlessly pursuing him, it was "God's good love" that followed him. "Surely goodness and mercy shall follow me all the days of my life" (Psalm 23:6). The word *follow* in this verse is a Hebrew verb (*radaph*) that is commonly used of predatory animals pursuing their prey. Yet, in a note of irony, David says it is God's faithful love that never stops reaching out to him. Consequently, he will stay close to Him, even when life gets tough. He will not turn his back on God because God will never turn His back on him. "And I will dwell in the house of the Lord Forever" (Psalm 23:6).

The most important thing to remember when you are in despair is that *you are never alone*. Jesus said, "I am with you always, even to the end of the age" (Matthew 28:20). He has compassion on those who are hurting. The Bible tells us, "When He saw the multitudes, He was moved with compassion for them, because they were weary and scattered, like sheep having no shepherd" (Matthew 9:36). On one occasion, Jesus encountered a widow whose son had just died. "When the Lord saw her, He had compassion on her and said to her, 'Do not weep'" (Luke 7:13). In the previous chapter, we discussed God's compassion as illustrated by the father in the story of the lost son. As the prodigal was returning home, "when he was still a great way off, his father saw him and had compassion, and ran and fell on his neck and kissed him" (Luke 15:20). God is a compassionate God, and He wants to heal not only your broken heart, but your broken soul as well.

> **God is a compassionate God, and He wants to heal not only your broken heart, but your broken soul as well.**

God is listening

When your heart is broken, never forget that God is listening. David said, "The eyes of the Lord are on the righteous, and His ears are open to their cry" (Psalm 34:15). Do you ever talk to yourself? It's a serious question. Sometimes when we are distraught and burdened beyond measure, we just start crying out for anyone who will listen; the thought that no one is listening only makes the pain worse. David reminds us that God is listening. He is there for us. We never have to worry that God will belittle us or chide us or mock us when we come to Him for help. When we are confused or need wisdom, He is waiting to calm our fears. The Bible says, "If any of you lacks wisdom, let him ask of God, who gives to all liberally and without reproach, and it will be given to him" (James 1:5).

For a number of years, I served as a professor at a college in a large metropolitan city. There were two Christian radio stations in the area, and they competed for listeners using various marketing campaigns. At one point, one of the stations had as its slogan, "God speaks." The implication was that through the music and ministry aired on their station, God would communicate His Word to listeners. Not to be outdone, the other station launched a campaign in which they assured everyone that "God listens!" That slogan was a bit of a double entendre. It was meant to remind listeners that God was approachable and available and attentive to our needs, yet it also implied that God listened to their station more than the competing station. DJs on both stations had a lot of good-natured fun ribbing each other about those slogans during that time.

The fact of the matter is that God speaks *and* God listens. He is not a God Who merely bellows out commands and directions through His Word. He is also a God Who hears our prayers, has compassion, and helps heal our broken hearts. When your heart is aching, it is hard to bring yourself to talk to anyone, especially if you think they are the source of your problem. Yet, as Peter reminds us, "The Lord is gracious" (1 Peter 2:2). David writes, "The Lord is gracious and full of compassion, slow to anger and great in mercy" (Psalm 145:8). Who better to talk to than someone who is gracious, gentle, and kind?

David said, "I have called upon You, for You will hear me, O God; incline Your ear to me, and hear my speech" (Psalm 17:6). Through His Word God speaks to us. "Open my eyes, that I may see wondrous things from Your law" (Psalm 119:18). God's comforting words are exactly what we need when we are hurting. "My soul melts from heaviness; strengthen me according to Your word" (Psalm 119:28). The psalmist declares, "Through Your precepts I get understanding… Your word is a lamp to my feet and a light to my path" (Psalm 119:104–105). Asaph, a Levite musician in the days of David, writes, "I cried out to God with my voice … and He gave ear to me" (Psalm 77:1).

Because God is listening, you should cry out to Him, no matter how counterintuitive it may feel at the time. God is not the enemy. God did not cause your pain. Quite the contrary! "The righteous cry out, and the Lord hears, and delivers them out of all their troubles" (Psalm 34:17). Who are you crying out to, to heal your broken heart? Who are you seeking? Are you seeking anyone? Or are you just walking around like a drunken person, clutching your chest?

A broken heart does not have to be fatal

Broken heart syndrome is a real medical condition. It is triggered by very stressful situations, like the death of someone you love. The medical name for this is *stress-induced cardiomyopathy*. The most common signs and symptoms of broken heart syndrome are chest pain and shortness of breath. You can experience these things even if you have no history of heart disease. Broken heart syndrome may be misdiagnosed as a heart attack because the symptoms and test results are similar. In fact, tests show dramatic changes in rhythm and blood substances that are typical of a heart attack; but, unlike a heart attack, there is no evidence of blocked arteries with stress-induced cardiomyopathy.

In broken heart syndrome, a part of your heart temporarily enlarges and does not pump well, while the rest of your heart functions normally or with even more forceful contractions. Researchers are just starting to learn the causes of this syndrome, and how to diagnose and treat it. Broken heart syndrome is usually treatable. Most people who experience it make a full

> **Whatever has caused your heart to break, God has the cure.**

recovery within weeks and are at low risk of it happening again. Similarly, on an emotional and spiritual level, a broken heart does not have to be fatal. "Many are the afflictions of the righteous, but the Lord delivers him out of them all" (Psalm 34:19). Whatever has caused your heart to break, God has the cure. There is no heartache that God cannot heal. It may hurt, even severely hurt; but it is not fatal.

We looked at the words of an anonymous psalm writer in Psalm 107 earlier. Let us take another look at that passage: "Their soul melts because of trouble. They reel to and fro, and stagger like a drunken man, and are at their wits' end" (Psalm 107:26–27). What does the rest of the passage say? "Then they cry out to the Lord in their trouble, and He brings them out of their distresses. He calms the storm, so that its waves are still" (Psalm 107:28–29). A broken heart does not have to be fatal. God will calm the storm.

The cure for a broken heart is supernatural. No medicine, no secular humanistic counseling, no self-help books, no pop psychology or power of positive thinking will mend a broken heart. Only God can; and when God is the doctor who is treating your broken heart, you can count on the fact that the remedy will be supernatural. David alludes to this when he refers to the "angel of the Lord" encamping around us. "The angel of the Lord encamps all around those who fear Him and delivers them" (Psalm 34:7). There is an unseen realm to life that is ever-present. Angels are God's "ministering spirits" (Hebrews 1:14). Even when there seems to be no way out, God can and will make a way. Jesus promised, "The things which are impossible with men are possible with God" (Luke 18:27).

"Once More unto the Breach, Dear Friend"

In Shakespeare's *Henry V*, there is a famous line that has become synonymous with idea of "Don't give up; try again." In Act III, the English have surrounded the French port of Harfleur. At first, the French army repels Henry and his troops, but Henry encourages them to attack yet again through a breach, or gap, in the wall surrounding the city. Passionately, he cries out to his men, "Once more unto the breach, dear friends, once more unto the breach!" If you are suffering from a broken heart; if you have been wounded and feel God cannot be trusted, let me encourage you to give God one more try. When you have no hope, come to the author of hope. Let "the God of hope fill you with all joy and peace in believing" (Romans 15:13).

There is a certain risk that comes with letting your guard down when you are hurting. Hurting people hurt people; and hurting people don't trust people. However, instead of recoiling inside yourself when your heart aches, the best and only solution is to cry out to God the way King David did. "I sought the Lord, and He heard me, and delivered me from all my fears" (Psalm 34:4). Some people will end up in hell because they were so hurt, they were unwilling to trust in the only One who could save them. You do not have to be one of those people. If you will let the hurt lead you to Him, He will mend your broken heart. Just trust Him. Put your faith in Jesus to save you and allow Him to give you His Spirit and mend your heart. "Once more unto the breach, dear friend!"

For Further Discussion

1. What does it mean to have a broken heart?

2. How does a broken heart prevent one from trusting God for salvation and eternal life?

3. Who do people often blame for the heartaches and trials in life?

4. Is God the cause of our pain and sorrow? Explain.

5. Is it okay to question God?

6. Can God be trusted?

7. Where do many people go to find help from their heartache?

8. Who really has the answer to life's sorrows?

8

Can You Hear Me Now?

How shall they believe in Him of whom they have not heard? And how shall they hear without a preacher?
—Romans 10:14

Cell-phone coverage has gotten progressively better as technology has advanced. However, in some rural parts of the country, such as the remote high Rockies in Colorado, a strong cell signal remains elusive. Whether you live in a densely populated area where cell service is pervasive, or you live in one of the remaining dead zones in America, everyone can relate to the struggle of trying to have a conversation on a mobile phone when the connection is patchy and inconsistent. We have all been there. Sometimes you catch only every other word; sometimes you keep talking for several minutes before realizing the call has been dropped; often there is an awkward and frustrating delay between when you say something and when the person on the other end of the line hears it. Communicating by cell phone, though convenient, is not always easy.

Verizon Wireless tapped into this shared experience of poor cell-phone connectivity in its famous ad campaign that ran from 2002 to 2011. In the TV commercials, a man on a cell phone shows up in various places across the country, such as secluded forests, busy city streets, office cubicles, corn fields, lonely dirt roads, and so on, asking, "Can you hear me now?" After a brief pause, the man smiles into the phone and says, "Good," indicating that the person on the other end of the line could hear him clearly. An announcer makes the point explicitly at the end of the commercial, "At Verizon, we're not satisfied until wherever you go, your call goes through." Whether true or not, Verizon's marketing strategy was successful in turning the question "Can you hear me now?" into a popular tag line, in much the same way that a Wendy's ad campaign in the 1980s made "Where's the beef?" a cultural catchphrase.

The ability to hear clearly is foundational if you want to talk by cell phone—or any phone for that matter. If you cannot hear, it poses a problem. Similarly, the Bible warms us that hearing the Gospel message is vital if you want to avoid hell. By "hearing," I mean being introduced to a specific message and understanding it. For most people, this means physically hearing the Gospel in a language they can understand. For some, such as those with hearing impairments, it might mean reading and comprehending the Gospel. Whatever the means of transmission, eternal salvation is obtained only by understanding and believing the good news that Jesus Christ, the Son of God, died and rose again to pay your personal penalty for sin. "He who believes in Him is not condemned; but he who does not believe is condemned already, because he has not believed in the name of the only begotten Son of God" (John 3:18). Jesus said, "Therefore I said to you that you will die in your sins; for if you do not believe that I am He, you will die in your sins" (John 8:24). Faith in Christ is the only means of salvation, and you cannot believe a message that you have never heard.

> **Faith in Christ is the only means of salvation, and you cannot believe a message that you have never heard.**

Dull Hearts

Henry and Elma had been married for fifty years, and their children decided to throw them a party for their golden wedding anniversary. The guest list included many relatives, friends, and neighbors. When the time came for Henry to stand up and toast his beloved wife of fifty years, he got everyone's attention, turned toward Elma, and said endearingly, "After fifty years, I've found you tried and true." Unfortunately, Elma was a bit hard of hearing and did not understand what her husband had said. "Eh? What did you say?" she replied. So, a little louder, Henry repeated, "After fifty years, I've found you tried and true." Still straining to hear, Elma said, "What's that? What did you say?" On the third attempt, Henry bellowed, "AFTER FIFTY YEARS, I'VE FOUND YOU TRIED AND TRUE!" Elma furrowed her brow and retorted, "Well, let me tell you something mister; after fifty years I'm tired of you, too!"

Quite often as our years increase, our hearing becomes dull. It can be more and more difficult to hear and understand what people are saying. Even the words of those we have loved and cherished for years can become imperceptible and incomprehensible. Unfortunately, the same thing is often true spiritually. Over time, the everyday din of life can drown out things of spiritual importance. This is true of the Gospel for many people. The voice of the Spirit convicting them of their sin and their need

Over time, the everyday din of life can drown out things of spiritual importance.

for a Savior can be hard to hear above the sounds of other worldly philosophies and endeavors.

The nation of Israel serves as a notable example of people who had trouble understanding the good news about God's plan of salvation. Almost immediately after being rescued from Egypt under Moses' leadership, they began to grumble and complain. Their ears were not attentive to God's message. Ironically, in the same way that Pharaoh would not hear God's message through Moses (Exodus 7:16), neither would the Israelites just days later. They often promised to listen and obey God's Word as revealed through Moses. They said to Moses, "You speak with us, and we will hear" (Exodus 20:19). However, their promises proved empty: Moses learned that the Israelites usually did not have "a heart to perceive and eyes to see and ears to hear" (Deuteronomy 29:4).

The problem with the Israelites was not so much that they could not hear; it was that they did not really understand what they were hearing. Just as a broken voice over a cell phone can be heard but not understood, God's people knew that a message was being delivered; their hearts were just too dull to understand it. This hearing problem persisted throughout the history of Israel up to and including the first century when they rejected the Messiah, Jesus Christ. God revealed through the prophet Isaiah that His people "keep on hearing, but do not understand; keep on seeing, but do not perceive" (Isaiah 6:9). He proclaimed that the hearts of His people were "dull," and their "ears were heavy," and their "eyes were shut" (Isaiah 6:10). Jesus often told the Jews of His day, especially the scribes and Pharisees, "He who has ears to hear, let him hear!" (Matthew 13:9). He quoted Isaiah when He declared, "Seeing they do not see, and hearing they do not hear, nor do they understand" (Matthew 13:13).

The Scandalon

Israel's dull heart became so severe that by the time Jesus arrived, even though He fulfilled Old Testament prophecy before their very eyes, they nevertheless viewed Him as a "rock of offense," and "they stumbled at the stumbling stone" (Romans 9:32 33). The word "offense" in this passage is the Greek word *skandalon*. It carries the idea of a stain or a disgraceful offense. It is where we get the English word scandal. The Jews knew that "anyone who is hanged is accursed of God" (Deuteronomy 21:23). Thus, when Jesus was crucified, it was scandalous to them. What they did not understand, however, is that by His death on the cross "Christ has redeemed us from the curse of the law, having become a curse for us (for it is written, 'Cursed is everyone who hangs on a tree')" (Galatians 3:13).

As some of their ancestors had throughout most of their history, many first-century Jews failed to trust God's plan of salvation by faith—in spite of the fact that the father of the Jewish people, Abraham himself, set the example when he was saved by faith (Genesis 15:6). It was also in spite of the fact that the message of faith was readily available to them (Romans 10:8).

> God told them through Moses that it was not too mysterious for you, nor is it far off. It is not in heaven, that you should say, "Who will ascend into heaven for us and bring it to us, that we may hear it and do it?" Nor is it beyond the sea, that you should say, "Who will go over the sea for us and bring it to us, that we may hear it and do it?" But the word is very near you, in your mouth and in your heart, that you may do it (Deuteronomy 30:11–14).

When Christ came, the Jews were expecting a Messiah who would be a victorious warrior and throw off the shackles of Roman oppression. They were looking for a King to "take the throne of His father David" (Luke 1:32), and "rule the nations with a rod of iron" (Psalm 2:8–9). They wanted Someone powerful whom they could follow and obey. Yet, the prophets of old had prophesied that the Messiah would have to suffer for the sins of the people. The cross had to come before the crown, humility before honor, tragedy before triumph. Likewise, faith must come before obedience.

Michael Card describes Israel's rejection of the Messiah well in his song "Scandalon":

> The seers and the prophets had foretold it long ago;
> That the long-awaited one would make men stumble.
> But they were looking for a king to conquer and to kill.
> Who'd have ever thought He'd be so weak and humble?

The song goes on to explain how the truth of the Gospel is hard for many people to believe, not just the Jews:

> He will be the truth that will offend them one and all,
> A stone that makes men stumble and a rock that makes them fall.
> ...

The idea that salvation is by grace, not works, is perplexing to many people. It offends our natural instincts to learn that we cannot earn eternal life through our own efforts. Michael Card writes,

> Along the path of life there lies a stubborn Scandalon.
> And all who come this way must be offended.
> To some He is a barrier, to others He's the way.
> For all should know the scandal of believing.
> ...
> It seems today the Scandalon offends no one at all.
> The image we present can be stepped over.

The idea that salvation is by grace, not works, is perplexing to many people. It offends our natural instincts to learn that we cannot earn eternal life through our own efforts.

Anyone who hopes to be rescued from the penalty of sin must embrace the cross. God's grace cannot be stepped over.

About seven hundred years before Christ, Isaiah predicted that the Jews would not believe it when their Messiah was sacrificed for the sins of the world. "Who has believed our report?" he wrote (Isaiah 53:1). Jesus would be "despised and rejected by men, a

Man of sorrows and acquainted with grief," and the people would "not esteem Him" (Isaiah 53:3).

> Surely He has borne our griefs and carried our sorrows; yet we esteemed Him stricken, smitten by God, and afflicted. But He was wounded for our transgressions, He was bruised for our iniquities; the chastisement for our peace was upon Him, and by His stripes we are healed. All we like sheep have gone astray; we have turned, every one, to his own way; and the Lord has laid on Him the iniquity of us all. He was oppressed and He was afflicted, yet He opened not His mouth; He was led as a lamb to the slaughter, and as a sheep before its shearers is silent, so He opened not His mouth. (Isaiah 53:4–7)

Jesus is the "lamb of God who takes away the sin of the world" (John 1:29). Peter reminds us that we are redeemed "with the precious blood of Christ, as of a lamb without blemish and without spot" (1 Peter 1:19). The Messiah became the Savior when He "Himself bore our sins in His own body on the tree … by whose stripes you were healed" (1 Peter 2:24). His sacrifice was not just for the nation of Israel; it was for everyone. "He is the atoning sacrifice for our sins, and not only for ours but also for the sins of the whole world" (1 John 2:2, NIV).

A Deafness Epidemic

The Jews were not the only ones who struggled to hear and believe the Gospel message. Gentiles had a difficult time hearing the Gospel as well. By the end of the first century, many Jews and Gentiles alike were deaf to the Gospel. John wrote, "He who is not of God does not hear us" (1 John 4:6). Late in his ministry, Paul told the Jews, "Therefore let it be known to you that the salvation of God has been sent to the Gentiles, and they will hear it!" (Acts 28:28). His point was that while many Jewish leaders in the first century continued to turn a deaf ear to the Gospel the way they had during Jesus' earthly ministry, perhaps the Gentiles would be more open to the Gospel.

Paul was right: many Gentiles heard and believed the Gospel. Many did not, however, demonstrating that spiritual deafness is a universal epidemic. Paul persevered in preaching the gospel until his martyrdom in 67 AD. He wanted as many people as possible to hear and believe the Gospel. In his last letter, he stated, "But the Lord stood with me and strengthened me, so that the message might be preached fully through me, and that all the Gentiles might hear" (2 Timothy 4:17). Two thousand years later, the church continues to proclaim that message so that all might hear.

The Bible is clear that faith is the only means of receiving eternal life. It is equally clear that faith can come only by *hearing*. "So then faith comes by hearing, and hearing by the word of God" (Romans 10:17). That means that faith for those who are lost and need to be saved comes by hearing the Word of God — namely, the Gospel. When you hear and believe the Gospel, you are born again. You receive the gift of eternal life and the indwelling Holy Spirit as a "deposit guaranteeing your inheritance" in heaven (Ephesians 1:14, NIV). Paul refers to the inseparable connection between faith and hearing in his letter to the Galatians. "This only I want to learn from you: Did you receive the Spirit by the works of the law, or by the *hearing of faith*?" (Galatians 3:2).

Jesus said, "Most assuredly, I say to you, the hour is coming, and now is, when the dead will hear the voice of the Son of God; and *those who hear will live*" (John 5:25). That Jesus was referring here to the spiritually dead receiving eternal life by faith is clear from the preceding verse. "Most assuredly, I say to you, he who hears My word and believes in Him who sent Me has everlasting life, and shall not come into judgment, but has passed from death into life" (John 5:24). Then, like today, there were those who heard but did not understand.

The Urgency of the Gospel

Because faith comes only by hearing, it is crucial that we share the Gospel message far and wide. Those who never hear the Gospel will spend eternity in hell. If never hearing the Gospel meant that a person was exempt from the penalty of sin, then the most effective way to keep people out of hell would be to stop sharing the Gospel! However, Jesus plainly commanded, "Go into all the world and preach the gospel to all creation" (Mark 16:15, NASB). Just before He ascended to heaven, where He sits at the right hand of the throne of God today waiting to return and establish His earthly Kingdom, Jesus said,

> **Those who never hear the Gospel will spend eternity in hell.**

"You shall be witnesses to Me in Jerusalem, and in all Judea and Samaria, and to the end of the earth" (Acts 1:8). No one has an excuse, even those who have never heard the Gospel. "For since the creation of the world His invisible attributes are clearly seen, being understood by the things that are made, even His eternal power and Godhead, so that they are without excuse" (Romans 1:20). Everyone must hear and believe the Gospel to escape the penalty of sin.

If the bad news that humankind is lost and headed to hell for eternity was all there was to it, that would be a problem. However, the bad news is not the *only* news. There is more to the story! The Gospel message in God's Word contains the good news that no one has to spend eternity in hell. Jesus died and rose again to pay your sin penalty. If you will simply trust in Him as the only One who can forgive sin and rescue you from hell, He will give you the free gift of eternal life. Jesus promises, "For God so loved the world that He gave His only begotten Son, that whoever believes in Him should not perish but have everlasting life" (John 3:16). "God demonstrates His own love toward us, in that while we were still sinners, Christ died for us" (Romans 5:8).

Paul asks an obvious question in his letter to the Romans, "How shall they believe in Him of whom they have not heard? And how shall they hear without a preacher?" (Romans 10:14). The word *preacher* here does not refer merely to a man of the cloth, one who serves as the pastor of a church; it refers to a "herald," that is, anyone who shares the Gospel. Before anyone can believe the Gospel, someone has to proclaim it. Quoting Isaiah 52:7, Paul writes, "How beautiful are the feet of those who preach the gospel of peace, who bring glad tidings of good things!" (Romans 10:15). Beautiful indeed.

Speak Up!

There is a saying, often attributed to St. Francis of Assisi (1182–1226), that goes like this: "Preach the Gospel at all times. If necessary, use words." There is no evidence that the thirteenth-century founder of the Franciscan Order ever made this statement. However, there is plenty of evidence that theologically the statement is dead wrong. It might be clever, and make for creative preaching, but it contradicts the clear teaching of the Bible. The implication of the saying is that the Gospel is more about how we live our lives than it is about what we say. Yet, as just discussed, the Gospel is something that must be heard and believed if it is to impart eternal life. Raking someone's leaves, or shoveling the snow on their driveway, or bringing them a meal when they are sick does not communicate the explicit message of the Gospel. These things are loving and kind, and they might provide an *opportunity* to share the Gospel, but these things in and of themselves are not the Gospel. The Gospel, by definition, requires words. As Duane Litfin, former president of Wheaton College, put it, "It's simply impossible to preach

> **The Gospel is something that must be heard and believed if it is to impart eternal life.**

the Gospel without words. The Gospel is inherently verbal, and preaching the Gospel is inherently verbal behavior."

Paul declares, "For I am not ashamed of the gospel of Christ, for it is the power of God to salvation for everyone who believes" (Romans 1:16). The Gospel is a message that must be believed in order for it to impart salvation. In order to believe the message, one must hear the message. "How shall they believe in Him of whom they have not heard?" (Romans 10:14). A belief that you are kind because you did a good deed for me may be well-founded, but that belief will not rescue me from hell. Remember, the Bible says that "Faith comes by *hearing*, and hearing by the word of God": namely, the Gospel (Romans 10:17).

When Cornelius summoned Peter to come share the Gospel with him, he was informed that Peter "will tell you *words* by which you and all your household will be saved" (Acts 11:13–14). The Bible says, "In Him [Jesus] you also trusted, *after you heard the word of truth, the gospel of your salvation;* in whom also, having believed, you were sealed with the Holy Spirit of promise" (Ephesians 1:13). Paul told the Corinthians that Christ sent Him "to *preach* the gospel," which he called the "message of the cross." Those who believe that message are saved (1 Corinthians 1:17–18). He goes on to say that it "pleases God ... through the message preached to save those who believe" (1 Corinthians 1:21). Later in the same epistle, Paul referred to "the gospel which I preached to you, which also you received and in which you stand" as "that *word* which I preached to you" (1 Corinthians 15:1–2).

When Peter appeared at the Jerusalem council with other early church leaders, Peter declared, "Men and brethren, you know that a good while ago God chose among us, that by my mouth the Gentiles *should hear the word of the gospel and believe*" (Acts 15:7). He later wrote, "Now this is the *word which by the gospel was preached to you*" (1 Peter 1:25). In Colossians 1:5, the Bible calls the Gospel the "*word* of truth." The testimony of Scripture is unambiguous. The Gospel requires words. These words must be *heard* and *believed*. What are these words? Jesus Christ, the Son of God,

The Gospel requires words.

died and rose again to pay your personal penalty for sin. If we want to share the Gospel, we must speak up! We must proclaim this message loud and clear.

Lewis Sperry Chafer put it eloquently when he correctly stated, "Preaching the Gospel is telling men something about Christ and His finished work for them, which they are to believe. This is the simplest test to be applied to all soul-saving appeals. The Gospel has not been preached until a personal message concerning a crucified and living Savior has been presented, and in a form which calls for the response of a personal faith." Some people end up in hell because they have not heard the Gospel. Perhaps you had not heard the plain and simple good news prior to reading this book. Let me ask you: "Can you hear it now?" Do you believe it?

For Further Consideration

1. Can you believe the Gospel message if you have never heard it?
2. What happens to those who have never heard the Gospel when they die?
3. How was Abraham saved eternally?
4. Can we share the Gospel message without using words?
5. What is the simple Gospel message?
6. What precisely must someone believe if they are to have eternal life?

9

Don't Believe Everything You Hear

Never before in human history has more bad information been available to more people.
— Scott Pelley, CBS News Anchor

In chapter 8, we discussed the importance of hearing the Gospel in order to believe it and be rescued from hell. There is a related issue, however, that has to be addressed as well. Some people end up in hell because they have believed a message that they *think* will get them to heaven, but in reality they have believed a *false* gospel. In other words, these people understand they are sinners in need of salvation; they believe the Bible has the answer to humankind's sin problem; they acknowledge the reality of salvation by faith alone; and they place their faith in a specific message in order to obtain salvation. Unfortunately, the information they received about how to be saved came

> **The world is more deceived today than it was yesterday, and it will be more deceived tomorrow than it is today.**

from Bible teachers who, wittingly or unwittingly, promoted erroneous gospel messages. Consequently, their faith is misplaced and will not result in their receiving eternal life. We must never forget that Satan is always blinding men's hearts to the Gospel (2 Corinthians 4:4), and one significant way that he does so is by promoting false gospels.

According to Mark Twain, "It is easier to fool people than to convince them they have been fooled." The evidence would seem to indicate he was right. Deception is at an all-time high. We know this anecdotally; more importantly, we know this biblically. The Bible tells us, "Evil men and impostors will grow worse and worse, deceiving and being deceived" (2 Timothy 3:13). This means that as time goes on, deception will become compounded. Deceivers will be deceived themselves and the overall state of truth will become worse with each passing year. The world is more deceived today than it was yesterday, and it will be more deceived tomorrow than it is today.

Satan himself is the great deceiver and his goal is to make sure the entire world remains "under the sway of the wicked one" (1 John 5:19). Jesus warned us about the devil. He said, "There is no truth in him. When he speaks a lie, he speaks from his own resources, for he is a liar and the father of it" (John 8:44). I have discussed the extent of Satan's influence on the world through the Luciferian Elite in some of my other books and DVDs. For the purposes of this present book, it is enough to be reminded that the fingerprints of Satan's co-conspirators are all over the place today. Indeed, the impact of deception can hardly be overstated in our current culture.

Deception is particularly noticeable when it comes to the accepted view of history, at least for those who take the time to study it. As more and more documents become declassified, and more and more credible information is leaked, we are learning that much of what we were taught in our compulsory government school textbooks is wildly inaccurate. Famed Russian author Leo Tolstoy reminded us, "History would be a wonderful thing if only it were true." Another Mark Twain truism asserts, "The very ink with which history is written is merely fluid prejudice." World leaders of the past and present have openly admitted that "history is written by the winners"—a quote often attributed to Winston Churchill, though its true origin is unknown.

The origin of another Winston Churchill statement is not in question. Churchill said, "History will be kind to me, for I intend to write it." Napoleon Bonaparte likewise admitted the fallacy of most accepted views of history when he said, "What is history, but a fable agreed upon." In other words, it is nothing for the power brokers of the world, in an attempt to advance their agendas, to manipulate history. It is a form of intentional confabulation, a manufactured Mandela Effect, if you will. Orwell reminded us, "Who controls the past controls the future; who controls the present controls the past." Which is why "those who cannot remember the past are condemned to repeat it," as George Santayana put it. We have very poor memories these days because our minds are cluttered with so much bad information. History is a fertile ground for deception; so too is everyday culture.

> We have very poor memories these days because our minds are cluttered with so much bad information.

The Internet and social media outlets have created a complex information superhighway where anything goes. Who determines what is true and what is false? How do we know what to believe? Does it even matter anymore? As author Steve Shahbazian put it, "It doesn't matter whether it's true, only that it's believable." "Fake news" is the newest buzzword to enter the sociopolitical arena. The term is bandied about like a birdie at a badminton tournament. News stories (and news networks), social media posts, books, and other materials that promote ideas with which someone disagrees are branded "fake news" by the thought police. Terms such as "post-truth" and "alternative facts" are forever etched in our minds, thanks to the 2016 presidential election.

Add to all of this the preponderance of *misinformation* and *disinformation* campaigns, as well as internet and social media trolls, sponsored by well-documented government programs like COINTELPRO, and it seems that finding the truth is nearly impossible sometimes. Many websites intentionally publish hoaxes and misleading information in an attempt to obfuscate or discredit the underlying issue; other genuine truth-seekers produce accurate documentaries and exposés that are labeled "fake news" or "conspiracy theories" by the real liars seeking to advance their deception. It is seldom about what it is about. Eric Blair, better known by his pen name George Orwell, warned us, "In an age of universal deceit, telling the truth is a revolutionary act." It is revolutionary precisely because it is so rare.

> ## It is seldom about what it is about.

There are layers of deception these days, which is why Mark Twain's observation that "It is easier to fool people than to convince them they have been fooled" is more profundity than tongue-in-cheek humor. In this lies-upon-lies culture, people have become wary of information they read online, see in a post, hear on the news, or read in a book. This state of widespread confusion has permeated the realm of Christianity to the extent that the precision and clarity of the Gospel have been severely damaged. The prevalence of deception is unmistakable evidence of Satan's ongoing attempts to blind people to the Gospel, and he uses false gospel

> ## The prevalence of deception is unmistakable evidence of Satan's ongoing attempts to blind people to the Gospel, and he uses false gospel messages as his most fiery darts.

messages as his most fiery darts (Ephesians 6:16). Lewis Sperry Chafer is even more blunt in his assessment. He calls these fiery darts "Satanic agents":

These Satanic agents are here, as before, described as those who seem to be teachers in the true faith, yet they bring in damnable heresies, in all covered subtlety, which crystallizes in a denial of the redemption that is in Christ. ...
[I]f the curtain could be lifted, their "angel of light" would be found to be Satan; working through them to resist the purpose of God; and themselves the ministers of Satan; speaking lies in hypocrisy; having their conscience seared as with a hot iron, daring in their exalted position to devitalize the Gospel of its power unto salvation, and dragging immortal souls after them into hell.

Chapter 4 discussed how many people end up in hell because they do not believe in one absolute standard of truth when it comes to the Gospel. In this chapter, we will discover that many people end up in hell not because they deny the existence of truth, but because they have believed the wrong "truth." "None are more hopelessly enslaved than those who falsely believe they are free" (Johann Wolfgang von Goethe, 1809).

No U-Turn Necessary

One of the more prevalent false gospels that has made its way into evangelicalism is the "U-turn" approach. Many people believe that getting into heaven requires some kind of a change of behavior. Even among those who think salvation is by faith alone, the idea that faith requires a behavioral "U-turn" is prevalent. It is not enough, they say, simply to believe the Good News. You must *repent and* believe." You must do an about-face and clean up your life before you can believe the Gospel and be saved. This view is built upon the concept of *repentance*, a word which certainly is found in Scripture. However, what does repentance really mean?

The idea that the words *repent* (verb) and *repentance* (noun) are inherently related to sin, though incorrect, has become the accepted view in many Christian circles. According to this erroneous view, *repent* and *repentance* are technical terms that always have the meaning of "turn from sin," or "stop sinning." Thus, when the Bible says, for example, that God is "not willing that any should perish but that all should come to repentance" (2 Peter 3:9), we are told this means you must "turn from all your sins and believe the Gospel." Some even suggest that "repentance of sins" and "faith" are "two sides of the same coin"; you cannot have one without the other, they say.

The famous Anglican scholar of the previous century, John Stott, is representative of this view. He insisted that repentance of sins is necessary for eternal life and defined *repentance* as follows: "Repentance is a definite turn from every thought, word, deed and habit which is known to be wrong." In a similar vein, John MacArthur writes, "Repentance is a critical element of saving faith … [I]t always speaks of a change of purpose, and specifically a turning from sin… a purposeful decision to forsake all unrighteousness…." He adds that "repentance [of sins] has always been the foundation of the biblical call to salvation," and states that "the gospel call to faith presupposes that sinners must repent of their sin and yield to Christ's authority." Another Reformed scholar, Mark Dever, concurs, "We must respond to this Good News by repenting of our sins and believing the Gospel if we would be forgiven by God, reconciled to Him, and saved from the wrath to come."

Is it correct to say that repentance is inseparably tied to the idea of "turning from sin"? This view, though widely held, is easily dismissed when we examine Scripture. Like all words, *repentance* must be understood in the context in which it is used. For example, if I asked you to define the English word *trunk*, you might say, "part of a tree," "an elephant's nose," "a large suitcase," or maybe "the storage area of a car." Unless and until you get the word *trunk* in context, you really have no idea what it means. If I said, "That elephant has a long trunk," the definition of the word becomes self-evident. Similarly, the words *repent* and *repentance* in Scripture do not have the same meaning in every occurrence, and they certainly do not always mean "stop sinning." To begin with, the Old Testament uses the word *repent* with reference to God. God "repented," we are told

> **Repentance is not a technical concept that is always inherently connected to sin.**

(e.g., Joel 2:14; Jonah 3:9). Of course, God never sins. Thus, we can conclude that repentance is not a technical concept that is always inherently connected to sin.

It is somewhat surprising that repentance has worked its way into the Gospel given the biblical data on the subject. The New Testament occurrences of the words repent (*metanoeō*, 34 occurrences) and *repentance* (*metanoia*, 22 occurrences) are remarkably scarce as compared to the occurrences of *believe* (*pisteuō*, 255 occurrences) and faith (*pistis*, 243 occurrences). As mentioned previously, eternal life is conditioned upon faith alone more than 160 times in the New Testament. The words repent and repentance collectively only occur nine times in the context of eternal salvation, and not one of these has anything to do with changing your behavior.

Moreover, the one New Testament book written specifically to tell readers how to have eternal life, the Gospel of John, does not use the words *repent* or *repentance* even a single time. John tells us that his account of the person and work of Christ was written "that you may believe that Jesus is the Christ, the Son of God, and that believing you may have life in His name" (John 20:31). If John's stated purpose was to show people how to have eternal life, and if repentance of sins was required to have eternal life, would it not makes sense for him to mention repentance somewhere in his Gospel?

What does it mean to repent, then? The word is a compound word in Greek that comes from *meta*, meaning *afterward* and *noeō*, meaning *I think*. The original idea was "to think afterward" or "to think again." If you look up the word in a Greek lexicon you will find that it means "to change the way one thinks," or "to change one's mind." Remember that meaning is always connected to context. Thus, when we see the word *repent* or the related noun *repentance* in Scripture we must ask, "Change the mind about what?" A careful search of the Bible will show that there is not a single passage where the words "repent of your sins" are used in the context of receiving eternal salvation.

As it relates to eternal salvation, repentance is limited to a change of mind about God or Christ. For example, Paul told the Ephesian elders that he was "testifying to Jews, and also to Greeks, repentance toward God and faith toward our Lord Jesus Christ" (Acts 20:21). Notice that he says nothing about sin here. His point was that a lost person must "change his mind about God," realize that only God can save him through His Son, and trust in Jesus for eternal life. Returning to Peter's statement that God is "not willing that any should perish but that all should come to repentance" (2 Peter 3:9), once again we see no mention of sin. Peter is simply saying that God wants lost people everywhere to "change their mind" about Him and receive the free gift of

> **As it relates to eternal salvation, repentance is limited to a change of mind about God or Christ.**

eternal life by faith alone. The idea is: "I used to think I could save myself (or I do not need salvation; or my works would save me; etc.), but I have *changed my mind*, and now I realize only Christ can save me; so I am trusting Him for eternal life."

Repentance means a "change of mind." It does not mean "turn from sin" or "change your behavior." Remember, the Bible says

God "repented," yet God never sinned. Some people will end up in hell someday because they have believed the erroneous idea that their eternal salvation is dependent upon their ability to make a U-turn, stop sinning, change their behavior, and clean up their lives. Sadly, they have believed the wrong message. The Bible knows nothing of this kind of Gospel message. You do not have to get cleaned up to take a bath. Simply come to Jesus in faith.

Give or Receive?

Another false gospel that has victimized people is the view that in order to avoid hell, you must give something to God. For instance, "give your life to God," or "give your heart to the Lord," and you will be saved. Some people will end up in hell because they thought their salvation could be obtained by giving something to God. Yet, as Charles Ryrie has pointed out, this kind of thinking "turns the Gospel 180 degrees in the wrong direction." Somehow, many people seem to have missed a fundamental element of the Gospel. Salvation is a gift, and God is the Giver; we are the receivers.

> **Repentance means a "change of mind." It does not mean "turn from sin" or "change your behavior."**

I think the idea that we must give something to God in order to be saved is influenced by the common practice of gift exchanges in our culture. At Christmas, Valentine's Day, anniversaries, and other occasions, we often trade gifts. If you give me something, I feel I should give you something in return. We speak of both items as "gifts"—and they are—yet the net effect is more like a

> **Some people will end up in hell because they thought their salvation could be obtained by giving something to God.**

give-and-take. If you give, I'll give. With eternal life, however, the gifting is in one direction only. When it comes to the Gospel, God gives; we receive.

Jesus said, "For God so loved the world that He gave His only begotten Son, that whoever believes in Him should not perish but have everlasting life" (John 3:16). Paul reminds us, "For the wages of sin is death, but the *free gift* of God is eternal life in Christ Jesus our Lord" (Romans 6:23). We are "justified *freely* by His grace through the redemption that is in Christ Jesus" (Romans 3:24). "Through one Man's righteous act the *free gift* came to all men, resulting in justification of life" (Romans 5:18). John explains that the gift of eternal life is received by believing in Christ. "As many as *received* Him, to them He gave the right to become children of God, to those who *believe* in His name" (John 1:12).

> **When it comes to the Gospel, God gives; we receive.**

Those who come to God with arms loaded full of offerings to give Him in the hopes that He will let them into heaven have missed the point. We have nothing to offer a holy God. In our sinful state, our only hope is for mercy and grace. Margaret Becker put it beautifully in her song entitled *Just Come In*. Taking on the voice of God in her lyrics, she writes,

> **What do I see**
> **You dragging up here**
> **Is that for your atoning?**
> **I wish you would**
> **Just come in**
> **Just leave that right there**
> **Love does not care**
> **Just come in**
> **Lay your heart right here**
> **You should never fear …**
> **I will forgive you**

No matter what you've done
No matter how many times
You turn and run
I love you
I wish you'd come

Some people will go to hell because, instead of believing the pure and simple Gospel message that salvation is a free gift paid for by the blood of Christ, they try to drag all manner of offerings to the altar and give them to God. God is the Giver, not the receiver; all He asks is that you come to Him in faith.

Knock, Knock!

A curious idiom developed within American evangelicalism around the turn of the twentieth century. Biblical phrases such as "trust in Jesus and you will be saved" and "believe in Jesus

> **The Bible never mentions the idea of "inviting Jesus into your heart" or "asking Jesus into your heart."**

and you will be saved," morphed into "invite Jesus into your heart and you will be saved." It was a strange development because the Bible never mentions the idea of "inviting Jesus into your heart" or "asking Jesus into your heart." Nevertheless, the notion that this is how one gets saved quickly spread and was reflected in the lyrics of several church hymns. Consider this 1898 Baptist hymn by Leila Naylor Morris, *Let Jesus Come into Your Heart.*

If you are tired of the load of your sin,
Let Jesus come into your heart;
If you desire a new life to begin,
Let Jesus come into your heart.
Just now, your doubtings give o'er;
Just now, reject Him no more;
Just now, throw open the door;
Let Jesus come into your heart.

In 1924, Harry Clarke wrote the little chorus, *Into My Heart*, which conveys the same idea:

> Into my heart, into my heart,
> Come into my heart, Lord Jesus;
> Come in today, come in to stay;
> Come into my heart, Lord Jesus.

Another well-known Baptist hymn, *The Savior Is Waiting*, was written by Ralph Carmichael in 1958. It too speaks of eternal salvation in the sense of inviting Jesus into your heart if you want to be saved.

> The Savior is waiting to enter your heart,
> Why don't you let Him come in?
> There's nothing in this world to keep you apart,
> What is your answer to Him?
> Time after time He has waited before,
> And now He is waiting again,
> To see if you're willing to open the door,
> Oh, how He wants to come in.

The message of these hymns represents quite a departure from the words of the following hymn written by John Stockton many years prior to the previous three. It is entitled, *Only Trust Him*:

> Come every soul by sin oppressed,
> There's mercy with the Lord.
> And He will surely give you rest
> By trusting in His word.
> Only trust Him. Only trust Him.
> Only trust Him now.
> He will save you. He will save you.
> He will save you now.
> For Jesus shed His precious blood
> Rich blessings to bestow;
> Plunge now into the crimson flood
> That washes white as snow.
> Only trust Him. Only trust Him.

Only trust Him now.
He will save you. He will save you.
He will save you now.
Yes, Jesus is the truth, the way,
That leads you into rest;
Believe in Him without delay,
And you are fully blest.
Only trust Him. Only trust Him.
Only trust Him now.
He will save you. He will save you.
He will save you now.

John Stockton penned these beautiful words in 1874. They accurately portray the simple message of the Gospel in God's Word. Many other hymns from the 1800s likewise emphasized faith as the only means of eternal life: songs such as "Faith Is the Victory," "My Faith Has Found a Resting Place," "'Tis So Sweet to Trust in Jesus," and "I Know Whom I Have Believed." By the end of the nineteenth century, though, the message in hymns shifted from "faith" to "Let Jesus come into your heart," then "Come into my heart, Lord Jesus," and then "The Savior is waiting to enter your heart, why don't you let Him come in?"

It's not possible to determine definitively whether the hymnology of the time reflected an already weakening theology or whether the enormous popularity of these hymns perhaps helped to shape and crystallize erroneous theology. Either way, the effect is the same. It was not long before altar calls and Gospel appeals in evangelical churches across America, particularly Baptist churches, were using "invite Jesus into your heart" as the go-to instructions for how to be saved. Over time, references to "faith" or "believe" became absent altogether. Children in Sunday school classes were asked, "Do you want to be saved?" If they answered "yes," they were told simply to pray, "Dear Jesus, Come into my heart. In Jesus' name, Amen." And with that, it was declared "You are saved!"

"Ask Jesus into your heart" became a shortcut—an abbreviated form—of a gospel message that is still prevalent to this day. Many preachers, evangelists, and lay soul-winners have replaced the one and only requirement of "faith in Christ" with "invite Jesus into your heart." Not only is this terminology not biblical, it is also very confusing. What does it mean, exactly, when we say, "Invite Jesus into your heart and you will be saved?" Many children are left puzzled by the meaning of these instructions, and, worse, go away with false assurance simply because they repeated a formula, "come into my heart." Such language, even if intended as a metaphor for "believe in Jesus," does not advance the clear and simple true Gospel message. Writers call such figures of speech "depreciating metaphors": they do not clarify, they confuse. Thus, they should be avoided, especially when it comes to a subject as important as how to have eternal life.

Why not use the biblical language? As mentioned previously, more than 160 times the New Testament conditions eternal salvation upon faith alone. There is nothing confusing about "believe on the Lord Jesus Christ and you will be saved." Everyone knows what it means to believe. There is no need to add ambiguous metaphors to the discussion of the Gospel. Some who use the "ask Jesus into your heart" model of presenting the Gospel have appealed to Revelation 3:20 for support. In that passage Jesus says to the

> **Many preachers, evangelists, and lay soul-winners have replaced the one and only requirement of "faith in Christ" with "invite Jesus into your heart."**

Laodicean church, "Behold, I stand at the door and knock. If anyone hears My voice and opens the door, I will come in to him and dine with him, and he with Me" (Revelation 3:20). However, in its biblical context this verse has nothing to do with eternal salvation. Jesus is speaking about fellowship, not salvation. He is speaking to those who are already saved within the Laodicean church. The passage says nothing about heaven, hell, eternal life, or salvation.

It is true that when a person trusts in Jesus alone for salvation, Jesus takes up residence in his heart. The Bible says, "That Christ may dwell in your hearts through faith" (Ephesians 3:17). However, to say that an unsaved person should "ask Jesus into his heart" in order to be saved confuses the *means* of salvation with one of the many *results* of salvation. At the moment a person places his or her faith in Jesus Christ, and Him alone, for eternal life, many spiritual events occur instantaneously and irrevocably in the life of the believer. To name just a few: We are born from above, declared positionally righteous in Christ, reconciled to a Holy God, sealed with the Holy Spirit of promise, and Jesus enters our heart, spiritually speaking. Yet all of these are the *result* of salvation by faith, not the *means* of it.

No one would suggest that we are saved by "asking God to declare us righteous," or "asking God to seal us with His Spirit," or "asking God to give birth to us from above." Why are so many people comfortable with mistaken notion that we are saved by "asking Jesus to come into our hearts"? Salvation is not a game of "Knock! Knock! Who's there?" Nowhere does Scripture ever indicate that we gain eternal life by "inviting" or "asking" Jesus into our hearts or lives. We are saved solely by trusting in the One who took our place on the cross, died and rose again, and offers to us forgiveness of sins and eternal life. If you have never done this, you will go to hell when you die, regardless of whether you "asked Jesus into your heart" or not.

Not All that Glitters Is Gold

There are many other distorted, flawed, and confusing "gospel" messages in Satan's arsenal. Ideas such as "forsaking your old ways," "praying a prayer," "publicly confessing Christ," and "surrendering to Christ as your Master and Lord" have all been put forth in various iterations from a variety of sources as the manner in which a person receives eternal salvation. None of these, however, are biblical. Throughout the Bible, the consistent, clear, and simple message is that salvation is only gained by faith. Gospel presentations that use phrases such as "Come to Jesus," "Give your life to Him," "Invite Him into your heart," and "Turn your life over to Christ" are vague and unhelpful and do not point people to faith alone in Christ alone as Scripture clearly does. Charles Ryrie cautioned, "Confusion abounds with respect to the content and presentation of the Gospel of the grace of God. Some do not present it purely; some do not present it clearly; some do not present it sincerely." We must endeavor to present the Gospel accurately because only the pure Gospel is "the power of God to salvation" (Romans 1:16; 1 Corinthians 1:17–18).

> **Throughout the Bible, the consistent, clear, and simple message is that salvation is only gained by faith.**

Some people dismiss these substantive differences over the essence of the Gospel message by appealing to semantics. They are willing to overlook sloppy, inaccurate presentations of God's plan of salvation because, they say, their purveyors mean well. "Does it really matter what words use," they protest, "as long as we are telling people about Jesus?" Yes. It matters. To borrow a metaphor from the Apostle Paul, "If the trumpet makes an uncertain sound, who will

> **The Gospel message in the Word of God is precise. It is clear. To depart from it when telling others how to be saved is to aid and abet Satan in his efforts to blind men's hearts to the Gospel.**

prepare for battle?" (1 Corinthians 14:8). Similarly, if the gospel message we are giving is inaccurate or unclear, how will people be saved? How will they know what to believe? "Faith comes by hearing, and hearing by the word of God" (Romans 10:17). The Gospel message in the Word of God is precise. It is clear. To depart from it when telling others how to be saved is to aid and abet Satan in his efforts to blind men's hearts to the Gospel.

Charles Ryrie was known as a masterful wordsmith. He could explain the most complex doctrinal issues in succinct, clear terms. Regarding the appeal that some people make to semantics, Ryrie states,

> How often I have heard the retort, "It's only a matter of semantics." In my experience it usually came from students using it as a defense mechanism to justify a poor answer to a question. And usually the question involved defining or explaining carefully the meaning of a biblical doctrine or concept. "A matter of semantics" was supposed to excuse fuzzy thinking and a poor, if not wrong, choice of words. Actually, semantics is not an excuse, nor is it incidental; it is the whole point. Semantics involves the study of meanings of words; so if one uses words which do not convey the meaning he or she is attempting to express, then a different meaning comes across.

"God is not the author of confusion," the Bible tells us (1 Corinthians 14:33). Satan, on the other hand, loves confusion. The devil "prowls around like a roaring lion, seeking someone to devour" (1 Peter 5:8). He blinds men's hearts to the Gospel by masquerading as "an angel of light" (2 Corinthians 11:14),

When it comes to the way of salvation, not all that glitters is gold.

even though he is a "ruler of darkness" (Ephesians 6:12). Because they are blinded by false gospel messages, when the light of the pure Gospel shines in the darkness, some people do not comprehend it (John 1:5). For this reason, many will end up in hell. When it comes to the way of salvation, not all that glitters is gold. Don't believe everything you hear. Simply believe in Jesus Christ, the Son of God, who died and rose again to pay your personal penalty for sin.

For Further Discussion

1. How has deception increased in our current culture? What are some tools for deception?

2. How does the prevalence of deception affect the Gospel message?

3. What is repentance and how does it relate to the Gospel?

4. Do we have to change our behavior in order to be saved?

5. Is there something we must give Jesus in order to be saved?

6. Is there a give and take to the Gospel?

7. Why is the concept of "asking Jesus into your heart to be saved" problematic? Does the Bible ever use this terminology?

10
Why?

"The world isn't fair, Calvin."
"I know, Dad, but why isn't it ever unfair in my favor?"
— Bill Watterson, "Calvin and Hobbes" (comic strip)

Ross Geller is one of six main characters in NBC's hit sitcom *Friends* that aired from 1994 to 2004. His PhD in paleontology from Columbia University positioned him as the most intelligent member of the group, but he was by far the goofiest as well. His hilarious escapades serve as the central theme of many of the show's episodes. In one scene, Ross has a meltdown after returning from a trip when he opens his suitcase to find that a shampoo bottle has leaked all over everything inside. He exclaims, in typical Ross-like hysteria, "Oh, no! Major shampoo explosion. Oh, no! It's all over everything. Why? Why me?" As he continues fumbling through his suitcase he cries, "Oh, no! Not another one! And this one is moisturizer! It's even harder to clean. Why? Why? Why do bad things happen to good people?"

When compared to all of the suffering in the world, Ross's little crisis hardly seems to warrant his over-the-top reaction—that's what makes the scene so funny. We can all relate to overreacting to a problem and making it seem bigger than it really is. A flat tire, a broken refrigerator, a shampoo bottle exploding in your suitcase ... these do not seem like issues that should prompt existential questions such as "Why do bad things happen to good people?" But what about more serious circumstances? Things like severe financial troubles, health problems, cancer, the loss of a loved one, divorce, and other painful life situations can challenge our ability to cope and make sense of the world.

Why do bad things happen to good people? Why is there so much suffering in the world? Why is there so much injustice? Why do the innocent die and tyrants thrive? *Why*, God? Questions like these are not uncommon in the collective consciousness when some unspeakable act of terror or horrific tragedy dominates the headlines. Yet, if we are honest, these questions do not arise only in the face of large-scale catastrophes. They sometimes make their way to the forefront of our minds in the privacy of our own daily lives. When we face personal difficulties and trials we are prone to ask, "Why?"

Painful circumstances that are beyond our control sometimes cause us to look heavenward and wonder, "Why, God?"

Painful circumstances that are beyond our control sometimes cause us to look heavenward and wonder, "Why, God?"

For many people this question is more than a fleeting, abstract contemplation that comes and goes from time to time. It can become a deep, lasting burden that plagues your thoughts all day and keeps you awake at night. Sometimes the question repeats itself over and over again until it drowns out all other thoughts. It can become paralyzing. Perhaps you are struggling with some of these questions right now. Like the psalmist, maybe your heart is crying out, "Why do You stand afar off, O Lord? Why do You hide in times of trouble?" (Psalm 10:1). "Why do You hide Your face, and forget our affliction and our oppression?" (Psalm 44:24).

Left to itself, despondency can come to define your whole outlook on life. It can taint every experience, every thought, and every decision. Eventually, bitterness toward God develops to the point that you cannot conceive of Him doing anything good. In chapter 7, we saw how some people reject the Gospel because of personal sorrow and a broken heart. This chapter focuses on the problem of suffering in general. Many people blame God for all of the pain and suffering in the world. They reject His Word and shun His free offer of salvation. Some people end up in hell because they cannot find a satisfactory answer to the question "Why?"

What kind of God would allow such pain and suffering in the world? This is a philosophical question that men and women much smarter than me have wrestled with through the centuries. The issue of suffering has been addressed by some of the greatest thinkers in human history, but with little satisfaction. The atheist Voltaire admitted, "One great use of words is to hide our thoughts." We can explain suffering, but we cannot understand it. Fortunately, we do not have to rely on the metaphysical musings of people like Plato, Kant, or Nietzsche when considering this question. We can look to a much higher and much more reliable source: the Bible, God's self-revelation to mankind, speaks directly to this issue.

> Some people end up in hell because they cannot find a satisfactory answer to the question "Why?"

The Blind Describing the Blind

The Apostle John's historical account of the life and ministry of Jesus Christ includes many events that are unique to his Gospel narrative. Indeed, ninety-three percent of the information revealed in John's Gospel is not recorded by Matthew, Mark, or Luke. One example is Jesus' encounter

> We can explain suffering, but we cannot understand it.

with a man who had been blind from birth. When Jesus stopped to talk to the blind man, His disciples asked Him a curious question. They asked, "Rabbi, who sinned, this man or his parents, that he was born blind?" (John 9:2). The disciples thought somebody must have done something wrong for this man to be blind. Either this man was being punished for something, or perhaps God had punished the man's parents by giving them a blind son. Either way, the disciples viewed life through the lens of cause and effect. God, they thought, is primarily retributive. When something bad happens, somebody must have done something to deserve it, or so they thought.

Jesus explains that this is not always the case. He said, "Neither this man nor his parents sinned, but that the works of God should be revealed in him" (John 9:3). In other words, God has a plan. The disciples were completely oblivious to the fact that God is much bigger than life's circumstances, and He is always at work accomplishing His purposes. Long before this man was born blind, God had a plan to use his condition to bring Himself glory and testify to the power of the Son of God so that many would believe in Him. The disciples' failure to see God's larger purpose in the situation amounted to little more than the blind describing the blind. Something more significant was at play, and the disciples were missing it.

> **God is much bigger than life's circumstances, and He is always at work accomplishing His purposes.**

Like Jesus' disciples, when we attempt to explain human suffering through the lens of our limited reasoning, we are approaching the problem from the wrong perspective. Instead of asking, "Why me?" we should be asking, "What, God?" "What are You doing in this situation?" Why is God allowing this? What is His plan in all of this? Even though we may not fully understand His plan, it is comforting to know that it is not about us; it is about Him.

Oh, the depth of the riches both of the wisdom and knowledge of God! How unsearchable are His judgments and His ways past finding out! "For who has known the mind of the Lord? Or who has become His counselor?" "Or who has first given to Him and it shall be repaid to him?" For of Him and through Him and to Him are all things, to whom be glory forever. Amen. (Romans 11:33–36)

Many people see life through the lens of retribution. When something bad happens, they ask, "What did I do to deserve this?" or "Why do bad things happen to good people?" They assume that life has some kind of master "fate regulator," where bad consequences are only the result of bad actions. As long as they do their part, they expect God to do what they think is His.

Cosmic Coke Machine

According to this faulty view of life, God is like a cosmic Coke machine. When we put in our coins, we expect to get what we requested. If we push the button for Dr. Pepper, we expect to get Dr. Pepper. If we push the button for Pepsi, we expect Pepsi. After all, we did our part. We put the money in the machine; we pushed the correct button. When we do not get what we expect, we become confused and angry. We push the button again; we start shaking the machine; we demand a refund. Why? Because we feel cheated. Some people have become so frustrated, when vending machines do not cooperate, that they shake them to the point that the machine topples over on them and severely injures or even kills them!

What we need to understand, however, is that God is not some kind of cosmic soft-drink dispenser. Life is not always fair, and it is not God's fault. He created a perfect world filled with justice, peace, and righteousness. We messed it up. God is doing everything He can to rescue us from the predicament we got ourselves into. He sacrificed His own Son in payment for our sins, and He offers freely to all the gift of eternal life. One day, according to His plan, He will make all things right in the world again. Jesus will return to the earth, establish His Kingdom, and there will be no more injustice and suffering. Until then, we must look to God as our hope in the midst of the storm, not point fingers at Him as if He were the storm-maker.

Life is not always fair, and it is not God's fault.

Faith is the key. What the disciples did not understand is that the blind man's condition was beyond his control. He was born that way. It certainly was not his fault, and Jesus made it clear that it was not the fault of the man's parents either. After Jesus healed the man, He asked him, "Do you believe in the Son of God?" (John 9:35). It is all about faith. It is not a matter of why something happened, it is a matter of "Who can fix it?" Some people become so obsessed with trying to figure out why something bad happened that they fail to look to the only One who can bring hope and peace. Doing so is like drowning in the ocean because you were so focused on figuring out why the boat capsized that you failed to grab hold of the life preserver that was right there beside you the whole time.

Reality Check

Suffering is a reality; but it was not that way from the beginning. God created the world in sinless perfection. The Bible tells us that when He was done, "God saw everything that He had made, and indeed it was very good" (Genesis 1:31). After man sinned, God said the earth was "cursed" (Genesis 3:17–19). Death entered the world just as God warned it would (Genesis 2:16–17). Thanks to us,

We must not allow suffering to influence our view of reality.

"[t]he whole world lies under the sway of the wicked one" (1 John 5:19). All of "creation groans and labors" (Romans 8:22), waiting for the final chapter in God's plan, a chapter when "God will wipe away every tear from their eyes; there shall be no more death, nor sorrow, nor crying. There shall be no more pain, for the former things have passed away" (Revelation 21:4). One day every bad chapter, every season of suffering, will end. For now, we live in a fallen world where Satan is prince. Consequently, sometimes bad things just happen to good people. Until Christ comes back and makes all things new (Revelation 21:5), this will be the case. In the meantime, we must not allow suffering to influence our view of reality.

Worrying about the reason for suffering will not accomplish anything. Sometimes only God knows the real reason, and He may or may not choose to show us until we get to heaven. The answer to suffering is faith, not worry. Jesus said,

> For this reason I say to you, do not be worried about your life, as to what you will eat or what you will drink; nor for your body, as to what you will put on. Is not life more than food, and the body more than clothing? Look at the birds of the air, that they do not sow, nor reap nor gather into barns, and yet your heavenly Father feeds them. Are you not worth much more than they? And who of you by being worried can add a single hour to his life? And why are you worried about clothing? Observe how the lilies of the field grow; they do not toil nor do they spin, yet I say to you that not even Solomon in all his glory clothed himself like one of these. But if God so clothes the grass of the field, which is alive today and tomorrow is thrown into the furnace, will He not much more clothe you? You of little faith! (Matthew 6:25–30)

Worrying cannot solve the problem of suffering any more than it can lengthen life, put food on the table, or put clothes on our backs. In fact, worry actually compounds the problem by creating physical and emotional difficulties that can lead ultimately to death. I heard one old preacher put it this way, "Ain't no use worryin' about the things you got no control over, 'cause if you got no control over 'em, ain't no use in worryin' about 'em. And ain't no use worryin' about the things you got control over; 'cause if you got control over 'em, ain't no use in worryin' about 'em." That advice is as simple as it is profound.

Though He Slay Me

When we allow suffering to turn us away from God, we are playing right into the devil's hand. This is precisely what he wants. For those who have never believed in Jesus Christ for salvation, suffering is one way that he blinds their hearts to the Gospel (2 Corinthians 4:4). Satan wants people to blame God for suffering instead of him. We learn this from the book of Job. In this book—possibly the oldest book in the Bible—the

When we allow suffering to turn us away from God, we are playing right into the devil's hand.

age-old problem of suffering is addressed. When Job faced unspeakable agony, his wife was a mouthpiece for Satan's game plan when she said to Job, "Do you still hold fast to your integrity? Curse God and die!" She viewed the suffering that Job and his family were facing as God's fault. Job, however, knew differently. He rebuked her and said, "You speak as one of the foolish women speaks. Shall we indeed accept good from God, and shall we not accept adversity?" (Job 2:9–10).

Job's faith was amazing. When his so-called friends suggested that Job must have done something to deserve his misfortune, he steadfastly maintained his faith in the Lord. "Though He slay me, yet will I trust Him," Job declared (Job 13:15). Job told the Lord, "I know that You can do everything, and that no purpose of Yours can be withheld from You" (Job 42:2). He understood that the regulating principle of life is grace, not retribution. Job was not being punished for something he had done, any more than the blind man that Jesus encountered was being punished for being blind.

It is true that sometimes actions have consequences; and yes, sometimes God does bless good and punish evil. Reaping and sowing are a natural part of life. "Do not be deceived, God is not mocked; for whatever a man sows, that he will also reap" (Galatians 6:7). However, contrary to what Job's friends were saying, God does not always operate this way. God rebuked Job's friends when He said to Eliphaz, "My wrath is aroused against you and your two friends, for you have not spoken of Me what is right, as My servant Job has" (Job 42:7). God is first and foremost a God of grace, not retribution.

> **God is first and foremost a God of grace, not retribution.**

A retributive view of God is appealing to many people because it enables us to feel we have some control over God, and we like to be in control. As Tom Constable put it, "If I can obligate God to bless me by being good, then God owes me something. Many people, of course, believe God owes them salvation because they are good people." They are wrong. The only thing mankind deserves is justice—eternity in hell. If the essence of life is: "Do good and you will be blessed; do bad and you will be punished," we become the masters of our own destiny. As discussed in chapter 5, however, this is not the case. If that was the essence of life, we would all be doomed to an eternity in a literal place of torment called hell, because no one can be good enough to merit God's forgiveness.

It is only by God's grace that "He has delivered us from the power of darkness and conveyed us into the kingdom of the Son of His love, in whom we have redemption through His blood, the forgiveness of sins" (Colossians 1:13–14). "Through the Lord's mercies we are not consumed, because His compassions fail not" (Lamentations 3:22). It is precisely because God is first and foremost a God of grace that no one ever has to go to hell. Anyone who in simple faith trusts in Jesus Christ and Him alone for forgiveness of sins and eternal life can be saved from the penalty of sin—namely, hell. It all comes down to faith.

What You See Is What You Get

In the early days of word-processing software, there was a difference between what the typist saw on the computer screen and what the printed copy looked like on paper. It is hard to imagine today, but back in the day, the computer screen was blue, and the letters were gray. What you saw as you typed had no resemblance to the final printed document. Formatting was accomplished by inserting certain codes in front of a section of text in order to make that text bold or italicized, for example. Even after inserting the appropriate formatting instructions, you could not tell by looking at the screen how the text would look when it was printed. If you wanted to know what formatting instructions you had inserted, you had to hit a function key that would reveal hidden codes.

For those who spend any time at all creating written documents using their computers, it was a glorious day when "WYSIWYG" was invented. WYSIWYG stands for *what you see is what you get.* The arrival of WYSIWYG meant that the information on the computer screen looked exactly like what it would when it was printed. Wouldn't it be wonderful if life was like that? Life would be much simpler if what we see represented an exact picture of what is really going on. This is not always the case. Sometimes there are things going on that are far beyond our comprehension. When tragedy strikes, or suffering comes like a flood, we sometimes stare blankly at life wishing there was a "reveal hidden codes" button to push so that we could understand what was happening more clearly.

> **Sometimes there are things going on that are far beyond our comprehension.**

In times of distress, we all want to know what is really going on. Yet, for reasons that remain a mystery, God has not allowed us to see all of life from His perspective. "For we walk by faith, not by sight" (2 Corinthians 5:7).

With life, what you see is not always what you get. There is more to life than what you can see, and feel, and touch. Some people end up in hell because they assume the worst when suffering comes knocking. They allow their pain to blind them to God's goodness and grace. Their focus is on what is seen, not what is unseen. When faced with intense heartache and incomprehensible hardship, they look at God and shake their fists and say, "Why me, God," instead of running to God for guidance and saying, "What now, God?" They bow up to God in bitterness instead of bowing down to Him in humility. Such a perspective might seem satisfying to a heart in search of someone to blame, but it will not satisfy the wrath of God in the day of judgment; only faith alone in Christ alone can do that.

Things Are Not Always as They Appear

Perhaps you have heard the story about the kindly old gentleman and his dog Sam. Sam was not the most attractive little mutt. In fact, he was rather ugly. Yet, his owner loved him very much, like the son he never had. Every Sunday this little old man would take his beloved dog Sam on a walk in the neighborhood park. One particular Sunday the man sat on a park bench with Sam at his feet, as was his custom midway through their walk, and began eating his sack lunch. Sam and his owner were not bothering anyone. They were minding their own business.

Soon a rebellious-looking young man appeared with his own dog. Both the youngster and his dog had a mean look to them — bulldog-type features to their faces. You could tell they were looking for a fight. Before long, the younger man and his bulldog began taunting the little old man and his ugly dog, Sam. "I bet my dog, Spike, could kill your ugly mongrel," the young man boasted loudly. Then he looked at his dog and said, "Sic 'im, Spike!"

The little old man, without flinching, calmly replied, "I wouldn't do that if I were you." Irritated by the old man's passive comment, the bully once again commanded Spike to attack the frail-looking pooch. The old man calmly repeated, "I wouldn't do that if I were you." As Spike lunged toward unsuspecting Sam, a battle ensued in cartoon-like fashion. There was a lot of barking, dust flew, and dogs ran in circles. When the dust settled the result was unexpected. Spike lay defeated, bloodied and torn to pieces by the ugly mutt. Humbled by the experience, the young bully looked at the gentle old man and asked, "Mister, what kind of dog is that, anyway?" The old codger replied, "Well, before I cut off his tail and painted him yellow, he was an alligator!"

How many times can you remember responding to a crisis, a situation, or some experience in your life only to find out later that things were not at all the way you perceived them to be? Every day we respond to life's circumstances based on how we see them. Those who see life through the lens of a retributive God are in danger of jumping into a dogfight that turns out to be an alligator fight because things are not always as they appear.

Those who see life through the lens of a sovereign, gracious God will trust Him even when things do not seem fair from a human perspective.

A review of the story of Joseph in the book of Genesis indicates that he learned this lesson well. Joseph lived by the motto: *Things are not always as they appear.* He understood that regardless of how things looked, God was at work accomplishing His purposes. Like Job, Joseph's outlook toward God was,

> Those who see life through the lens of a sovereign, gracious God will trust Him even when things do not seem fair from a human perspective.

"I know that You can do everything, and that no purpose of Yours can be withheld from You" (Job 42:2). Like David, Joseph believed, "As for God, His way is perfect; the word of the Lord is proven; He is a shield to all who trust in Him" (Psalm 18:30).

Joseph was the eldest son of Jacob and Rachel and Jacob's eleventh son in all. His father loved him more than all of his brothers. This caused his brothers to hate him. Their jealousy was aggravated by Jacob's overt expression of favoritism in giving Joseph a beautiful, colorful coat. Every time his brothers saw Joseph wearing that coat, they were reminded of his preferred status with their father. Acting out of jealousy and hatred, his brothers—with the exception of Reuben—resolved to kill him. Reuben intervened on Joseph's behalf and persuaded them to cast Joseph into a pit instead. While the brothers were eating, a company of Arabian merchants came on the scene and Joseph was sold to them for twenty shekels of silver.

This was the first in a series of bad breaks and unfair life circumstances that Joseph would be called upon to endure. In the years to follow he found himself in jail, falsely accused, and frequently mistreated. Yet, through it all, he kept the right perspective. He knew that something bigger and greater was at work. He knew that things are not always as they appear. Many years later, Joseph found himself in a position of power and authority in Egypt. When his father, Jacob, died, his brothers feared that Joseph would seize the opportunity to exact revenge on them for their evil deeds, but he did not.

Joseph's response to his brothers is one of the most surprising statements in the entire Bible. Joseph said, "Do not be afraid, for am I in the place of God? But as for you, you meant evil against me; but God meant it for good, in order to bring it about as it is this day, to save many people alive" (Genesis 50:20). Joseph knew that even though what happened to him was not good or pleasant—and in fact was extremely painful—it was all part of God's sovereign plan to accomplish a greater purpose. Jesus exemplified the same attitude Himself during a time of intense suffering—the worst suffering any human being has ever experienced. Just hours before He died a cruel death on the cross, and knowing what was ahead, He cried out in anguish to God and said, "O My Father, if it is possible, let this cup pass from Me; *nevertheless, not as I will, but as You will*" (Matthew 26:39). He recognized God's plan and accepted it by faith.

> **God is always looking out for your best interest even if you cannot see how.**

Can you say that today? If you find yourself struggling with difficult circumstances or life experiences; if you find yourself asking "Why?," never forget: *Things are not always as they appear.* God is always looking out for your best interest even if you cannot see how. Do not allow your suffering, no matter how painful, to keep you from believing in the One who took

your place on the cross and is the only One who can save you:
Jesus Christ.

For Further Discussion

1. Why is there so much suffering in the world?
2. Is God to blame for this suffering?
3. What do we mean when we talk about a retributive view of God?
4. What is God's primary operating principle?
5. Do we always reap what we sow? Explain.
6. Where should we turn when life does not make sense?
7. What does it mean to walk by faith and not by sight?
8. How should we respond when life is not fair?

11

Busyness

Life's but a walking shadow, a poor player
That struts and frets his hour upon the stage
And then is heard no more.
It is a tale told by an idiot,
Full of sound and fury,
Signifying nothing.
—William Shakespeare, *Macbeth*, Act V, Scene 5

In her book, *Overwhelmed: Work, Love, and Play When No One Has the Time* (2014), Brigid Schulte makes the undeniable case that we are busier today than at any other time in human history. She writes, "Busyness has become such a social value that we will even create it; we will create that sense of breathlessness because we think that's how we show status and importance. That is a really interesting and troubling finding." One would think that given all of the advances in technology over the past two decades, there would be more automation resulting in more free time. Yet, as Schulte points out, this is not the case. It is just the opposite, she suggests:

> What's happening now with technology is we live with very porous boundaries. All those little interruptions fragment our time and attention and make us feel like work never ends. It makes us feel like we don't ever have that sacred time for family or to breathe or meditate or for leisure. Time is contaminated for everyone.

According to *Forbes* writer Meghan Casserly, phrases such as "swamped," "crazed," "overloaded," or "hasn't seen daylight in weeks" dominate our conversations. Being busy has become a game of one-upsmanship. Casserly points out:

> A full Outlook calendar seems to have replaced the sports car as the new status symbol. Being busy means you're important, needed, valued. Time isn't just money, it's the red Jaguar, the Birkin bag and the private jet all rolled into one. Have no time? Honey, you've arrived.

New York Times writer Tim Kreider calls it the "busy trap." "If you live in America in the 21st century," Kreider writes, "you've probably had to listen to a lot of people tell you how busy they are. It's become the default response when you ask anyone how they're doing: 'Busy!' '*So* busy.' '*Crazy* busy.'"

It was not supposed to be like this. Scientific and technological advances were supposed to bring *more* leisure time, not less. As Kerby Anderson puts it, "Optimistic futurists in the 1950s and '60s, with visions of utopia dancing in their heads, predicted Americans would enjoy ample hours of leisure by the turn of the century." According to Anderson, testimony before a Senate subcommittee in 1967 predicted that in the not-too-distant future, people would be working just "twenty-two hours a week" and "twenty-seven weeks a year," and "would be able to retire at age thirty-eight." Clearly, that has not happened. What has all of this busyness gotten us?

What has all of this busyness gotten us?

Sound and Fury

Life these days reminds me of a line from *Macbeth*. After learning that the queen is dead, in perhaps the most well-known of all Shakespearean soliloquies, Macbeth says,

She should have died hereafter;
There would have been a time for such a word.
—To-morrow, and to-morrow, and to-morrow,
Creeps in this petty pace from day to day,
To the last syllable of recorded time;
And all our yesterdays have lighted fools
The way to dusty death. Out, out, brief candle!
Life is but a walking shadow, a poor player
That struts and frets his hour upon the stage
And then is heard no more. It is a tale
Told by an idiot, full of sound and fury
Signifying nothing.

—Act V, Scene 5

The question is: *What does all of our sound and fury signify?* How much of our sound and fury actually produces something of value? Busyness does not always equate to productivity. Indeed, it can be a distraction. It is one thing for busyness to distract from ordinary priorities, such as mowing the lawn, cleaning the house, or eating a good dinner. However, when busyness starts to steal our attention from things of eternal value, it is another matter altogether. No matter how well you prioritize your earthly life, if you ignore the life to come, it will "signify nothing" at the final judgment.

Jesus addressed this contrast between earthly priorities and heavenly priorities during a visit to the home of two sisters, Mary and Martha. During his stay, Martha attended to the many tasks that come with having guests in your home. Meanwhile, Mary "sat at Jesus' feet and heard His word" (Luke 10:39). Eventually, Martha became bothered by Mary's lack of help with the chores and asked Jesus, "Lord, do You not care that my sister has left me to serve alone? Therefore, tell her to help me" (Luke 10:40). Jesus' answer is instructive. He said, "Martha, Martha, you are worried and troubled about many things. But one thing is needed, and Mary has chosen that good part, which will not be taken away from her" (Luke 10:41–42).

In other words, according to Jesus, spiritual matters take precedence over earthly matters. Mary was focused on the Son of God who was in her midst; everything else was insignificant by comparison. Sometimes the tyranny of the urgent causes us to neglect the urgency of the transcendent. In our busyness, we forget that there is more to life than what we can see, and feel, and touch. This is yet another way that Satan blinds men's hearts to the Gospel (2 Corinthians 4:4). He convinces

> **Sometimes the tyranny of the urgent causes us to neglect the urgency of the transcendent.**

people that issues related to heaven, hell, and the afterlife are not important. When the Holy Spirit brings conviction about sin and the need for a Savior, His message is drowned out by the clamor and clatter of earthly life. Consequently, many people put off believing the Gospel message until it is too late and end up spending eternity in hell.

Time Flies

Have you ever heard the phrase "full of life"? When someone is full of life, it means they are making the most of life, enjoying every moment. They cannot wait to get out of bed every morning. You have probably also heard the phrase, "Your days are numbered." It means there is a limit to how much life you will live. No matter how much you are enjoying life, no matter how full of life you may be, no matter how busy you are, every life comes to an end. Someone has pointed out that life's ultimate statistic is the same for everyone: *One* out every *one* dies.

Like many common English idioms, the phrase "Your days are numbered" originates from the Bible. In Psalm 90, Moses says to the Lord, "So teach us to number our days, that we may gain a heart of wisdom" (Psalm 90:12). In other words, be aware of the limited nature of your life and make the most of every day. The New Testament repeats this principle when it tells us to "redeem the time" (Ephesians 5:16; Colossians 4:5). The Greek word translated "redeem" is *exagorazō*, which means, "rescue from loss." Once a day is spent, you can never get it back. It is lost forever. Geoffrey Chaucer reminded us, "Time and tide wait for no man," by which he meant that no one is so powerful that he can stop the progress of time. Similarly, we might say time owes no man. You cannot deposit a single minute in the bank of time to have it repaid at a later date.

> You cannot deposit a single minute in the bank of time to have it repaid at a later date.

Time is a funny thing. As you get older, your perspective on time changes. For children, each new day is a whole new world. It is filled with adventures, wonder, and excitement, and each day lasts a long, long time to a child. Six months takes forever to a child, but to an adult that span can go by in the blink of an eye. What's in a life? On average, Americans can now expect to live 78.7 years, a statistically significant drop of 0.1 year, according to a report published by the National Center for Health Statistics in 2018. Women can now expect to live a full five years longer than men: 81.1 years versus 76.1 years.

A study done in 2016 took a look at the life of an average person in terms of pure numbers. Researchers surveyed more than 9,000 people. They totaled up the amount of time we spend doing various things and converted the time to days. What they found was pretty interesting. An average lifetime consists of 28,689 days (78 years). In that time, the average person will spend 11,762 days looking at a digital screen of some type—41% of their total life. The average person will spend 8,521 days sitting down (29.7%); 1,951 days socializing with others (6.8%); and, embarrassingly, only 198 days exercising (0.69%). In a lifetime, the average person can expect to laugh 554,024 times, spend a year and a half looking for misplaced items, spend six years waiting in lines, and receive 1,000 advertising messages each day. In a typical lifetime, you could climb Mount Everest 5.1 times or run the circumference of the world 2.2 times.

The Wisdom of Experience

Returning to Psalm 90, the superscription tells us it is "A Prayer of Moses the Man of God." This psalm is the oldest of all psalms in the Bible. Moses wrote it near the end of his wilderness wanderings in approximately 1406 BC. In it, he gives us several thoughts on the temporal, fleeting nature of life from the perspective of a wise old man. Moses exemplified the principle found in Proverbs, "He whose ear listens to the life-giving reproof will dwell among the wise" (Proverbs 15:31, NASB). He certainly had plenty of life experience from which to draw life's lessons. The word day or its equivalent is used nine times in this short psalm. Moses asks God for heavenly wisdom in view of life's brevity. His theme in this psalm is: We're only here for a little while; therefore, make it count. The key verse is "So teach us to number our days, that we may gain a heart of wisdom" (Psalm 90:12).

According to Moses, the purpose of numbering our days is to gain a heart of wisdom so that we will be able to live life skillfully. The word *wisdom* used in this verse is the Hebrew word chokmah. It is used 149 times in the Old Testament. Usually it is translated "wisdom," but occasionally "skill" or "craftsman[ship]." *Chokmah* originally denoted the possession of a specific skill such as tailoring, metallurgy, building, farming, and the like. Over time, it came to be associated with "skill at living life" in general. Thus, a person with "a heart of wisdom" is a person "skilled at living life." By making the most of every day, Moses tells us, we will become more skilled at living life.

Numbering our days begins by realizing that our days are limited. Moses contrasts the eternality of God with the temporality of man. Of God, Moses writes, "Lord, You have been our dwelling place in all generations. Before the mountains were brought forth, or ever You had formed the earth and the world, even from everlasting to everlasting, You are God" (Psalm 90:1–2). Of man, Moses writes, "You turn man to destruction" (Psalm 90:3). Man dies; God does not. Because our days are limited, it makes sense to prioritize our activities. Why waste time on things of little or no value?

On Death and Dying

Moses was able to prioritize life because he understood death. According to the Bible, there were 600,000 men in the Exodus when Moses led the Israelites out of Egypt. It is likely that there were more women than men in the Exodus, but let us assume for simplicity that there were also 600,00 women. That means that Moses led 1.2 million adults, not counting children, out of Egypt. All but two of these people died during the next forty years in the wilderness. If we do the math, that means an average of eighty-seven people died per day; that's three or four people every hour! Moses lived in an environment of death. If he had written an autobiography, a good title would be On Death and Dying. He understood the perspective that man's days are limited. He understood that our bodies are frail. He understood that when you get right down to it, this old planet we call Earth is just one, giant, round cemetery. "To ignore this reality," Bruce Waltke said, "is to live in a fool's paradise." That is why an understanding that our days are limited makes one wise.

In our culture today, we camouflage the process of death. We seek to make it pretty and dignified and convenient by things like euthanasia and abortion; but disguising the ugliness of death no more eliminates it than putting flowers on a headstone eliminates the grave beneath it. Even Christians are guilty, sometimes, of overemphasizing the immortality of the soul and underemphasizing the frailty of life. We need to realize that our days are limited. David wrote, "Lord, make me to know my end, and what is the measure of my days, that I may know how frail I am. Indeed, You have made my days as handbreadths, and my age is as nothing before You; certainly every man at his best state is but vapor" (Psalm 39:4–5).

Ethan the Ezrahite put it this way, "Remember how short my time is; for what futility have You created all the children of men? What man can live and not see death? Can he deliver his life from the power of the grave?" (Psalm 89:47 48). Death is the great equalizer. The Bible reminds us, "It is appointed for men to die once, but after this the judgment" (Hebrews 9:27). Solomon, the wisest man who ever lived, understood the reality of death even better than Moses. "For what happens to the sons of men also happens to animals; one thing befalls them: as one dies, so dies the other" (Ecclesiastes 3:19). No one can escape death. This reality should affect the way we live.

Numbering Our Days

How do we number our days? Not only should we realize that our days are limited, but also we must realize that every day is precious. Moses goes on to point out that because our days are limited, they are very precious. He uses five analogies to describe the value of a day. First, Moses says a thousand years is like 24 hours relative to eternity. He writes, "For a thousand years in Your sight are like yesterday when it is past" (Psalm 90:4). To understand the significance of this, let's do some math. Since none of us will live to be a

> No one can escape death. This reality should affect the way we live.

thousand years old, let's reduce that number to 100 to make the math easier. Let's be optimistic and assume we live to be 100 years old. That's one-tenth of 1,000. So, using Moses' analogy, if we live to be 100 years old, our entire life is like one-tenth of 24 hours, or 2.4 hours relative to eternity. At best, our lifetime is like 2.4 hours!

However, Moses does not stop there. He says that really, a thousand years is like "a watch in the night" (Psalm 90:4). A watch was four hours long. Thus, a thousand years is like four hours relative to eternity. But again, we don't live to be a thousand, so let's translate that to our life. Again, assuming we live to be 100, our life is like one-tenth of 4 hours, or 24 minutes! At best, our lifetime is like 24 minutes!

Moses is not done yet. He uses yet another analogy to illustrate the fleeting nature of life, comparing a thousand years to a flood. He says, "You carry them away like a flood" (Psalm 90:5). Our years are carried away, one after the other, like waves carry away water, Moses tells us. One generation after another is swept away like the waves of the sea. How long does it take between waves? Have you ever been to the ocean? I am told that it takes on average about 90 seconds at the most from one wave to the next. So, a thousand years is like 1.5 minutes! Which means our lives are like one-tenth of a minute and a half: that's nine seconds! At best, our lifetime is like nine seconds!

Next Moses compares a thousand years to sleep. He says, "They are like a sleep" (Psalm 90:5). Now this is interesting, because sleep is really timeless from our perspective. You go to sleep and then you wake up and it is as if it all happens in the blink of an eye. Of course, we know that six to eight hours have passed, but it is as if it happens while time stands still. Thus, a thousand years is like the blink of an eye. Which means our 100-year life is like a one-tenth of a blink of an eye; 100 years is like a fraction of a second. At best, our lifetime is like a fraction of a second!

Moses concludes with the analogy of grass, which grows up and withers while no one is watching. He tells us that a thousand years are like "grass which grows up. In the morning it flourishes and grows up; in the evening it is cut down and withers" (Psalm 90:5–6). Grass, like all vegetation, grows while no one is looking. Seldom do you get the opportunity to watch a flower, for example, open up in the spring. You just see a bud and think that any day now that flower is going to be open. One

> **Even a single day is a gift from God because they all belong to Him.**

day, you walk by and there it is. You think, "Wow! What a pretty flower." It all happens automatically, while no one is looking; and it is gone before you know it. Life is like that, Moses says. It is what happens while you are not watching, and it is gone before you know it. Every day is precious. "For what is your life? It is even a vapor that appears for a little time and then vanishes away" (James 4:14).

We number our days by realizing that our days are limited, every day is precious, and also that every day belongs to God. Moses writes:

> For we have been consumed by Your anger, and by Your wrath we are terrified. You have set our iniquities before You, our secret sins in the light of Your countenance. For all our days have passed away in Your wrath; we finish our years like a sigh. The days of our lives are seventy years; and if by reason of strength they are eighty years, yet their boast is only labor and sorrow; for it is soon cut off, and we fly away. (Psalm 90:7–10)

Moses points out that man's sinfulness has aroused God's wrath. It separates us from God. In fact, it is our sinfulness that brought death into the world in the first place (Romans 5:12). Even a single day is a gift from God because they all belong to Him. We own none of them. All we deserve is death. Our "days pass away" because of our sin. In fact, Moses says that the normal human lifespan is seventy years. For some it might even be eighty years. Nevertheless, at some point life ends, because the "wages of sin is death" (Romans 6:23).

We do not live our days independent of God. We live them by His grace and by His mercy. He is directly and immediately involved in our day-to-day lives. Most people live like the Israelites in the wilderness, just killing time. The Israelites were guilty of unbelief, a lack of faith. Moses says that we should go through life numbering our days and acknowledging God's presence and sover-eignty. Numbering our days means having the right perspective and attitude toward life: There is a God; you are not Him.

There is a God; you are not Him.

David wrote, "Indeed, You have made my days as handbreadths, and my age is as nothing before You; certainly every man at his best state is but vapor" (Psalm 39:5). Many people will face death someday realizing they wasted their entire life on earthly things. God wants us to receive the free gift of eternal life by faith alone in Christ alone; and, from that point forward, live our earthly lives recognizing that what matters most is not what we can see, and feel, and touch.

Excuses, Excuses

Those who do not understand the value of a day may soon become too distracted to see the big picture. Busyness causes us to waste time, not redeem it. Busyness creates priorities that are out of balance. Jesus was having dinner one time in the home of one of the rulers of the Pharisees when he told an interesting parable.

It is often referred to as the "Parable of the Great Supper." His story illustrates the dangers of busyness.

> A certain man gave a great supper and invited many, and sent his servant at supper time to say to those who were invited, "Come, for all things are now ready." But they all with one accord began to make excuses. The first said to him, "I have bought a piece of ground, and I must go and see it. I ask you to have me excused." And another said, "I have bought five yoke of oxen, and I am going to test them. I ask you to have me excused." Still another said, "I have married a wife, and therefore I cannot come." So that servant came and reported these things to his master. Then the master of the house, being angry, said to his servant, "Go out quickly into the streets and lanes of the city, and bring in here the poor and the maimed and the lame and the blind." And the servant said, "Master, it is done as you commanded, and still there is room." Then the master said to the servant, "Go out into the highways and hedges, and compel them to come in, that my house may be filled. For I say to you that none of those men who were invited shall taste my supper" (Luke 14:16–24).

The point Jesus was making was that the nation of Israel had been invited to receive her King, and yet, because the focus of the Jewish leaders was on earthly things such as status, power, legalistic rules, and politics, many of them missed it. The scribes and Pharisees were so busy doing things they thought were important that, like Mary's sister Martha, they failed to recognize the presence of the Son of God in their midst. That the "great supper" in the parable represents the eternal Kingdom is unmistakable.

In the parable, all of the invited guests declined the invitation and made excuses as to why they could not come. One allowed his real estate transactions to keep him from accepting the invitation. Another had farm work to do. Still another blamed it on his wife — an excuse that undoubtedly has been used countless times down through the ages! Each of these excuses amounts to nothing more than a failure to prioritize. The invited guests did not feel that the banquet, no matter how grand, was worthy of their attention. When the invited guests would not come, the host opened the guest list to include others. As is often the case with His stories, Jesus juxtaposed the self-righteous, upstanding members of society with those who were deemed less worthy. The new invitees included "the poor, the maimed, the lame, and the blind." Anyone who wanted to come could come.

As with the great supper, so also with heaven. The invitation has gone out to the entire world. Jesus said, "Come to Me, all you who labor and are heavy laden, and I will give you rest" (Matthew 11:28). The last chapter of the Bible contains a universal invitation, "Whoever desires, let him take the water of life freely" (Revelation 22:17). Only those who *by faith* accept the free gift of eternal life will be in heaven someday. Those who receive the invitation but ignore it will not. "Facts do not cease to exist because they are ignored," as Aldous Huxley reminded us. Heaven and hell are facts; they are realities. Some people will go to hell when they die because they are too distracted, too busy, or otherwise disinterested to respond to God's invitation.

For Further Consideration

1. How has technology made us busier?

2. What does it mean to redeem the time?

3. What does it mean to number your days?

4. In what ways does busyness distract us from the Gospel?

5. How does the reality of death create urgency for the Gospel?

6. Why do some people make excuses when it comes to spiritual matters?

7. Who is on heaven's guest list? Will all of the invited guests come?

8. How do you avoid hell and gain eternal life in heaven?

12

Come One, Come All!

Come every soul by sin oppressed,
There's mercy with the Lord,
And He will surely give you rest
by trusting in His word.
Only trust Him, only trust Him,
Only trust Him now.
He will save you. He will save you.
He will save you now.
—John H. Stockton (1874)

"Come one, come all!" is an old English idiom. It was an advertising slogan associated with public events and performances. The slogan essentially amounted to both an invitation and a promise. The invitation is easy to see. "Come!" Notices were hung far and wide inviting people to a particular show. Posters often showcased the stars of the show and teased certain features to entice people to attend. "Come to our event! Everyone is welcome! It is going to be great!" In the days before the Internet and social media, print advertising was crucial to the success of any production.

Implicit within each such invitation was also a guarantee: If you travel to this event, we promise you it will go on as scheduled. Travel was quite difficult two or three hundred years ago, and people would not come to an event if they feared it would be cancelled for any of a variety of reasons (weather, poor attendance, etc.). No one wanted to spend the time and money necessary to travel only to find out that their efforts had been wasted. "Come one, come all!" assured each potential attendee that even if he was the only one who came to the performance, the show would go on. Providing such an assurance on advertising pamphlets helped to boost attendance at an event.

Similarly, the message of the Gospel serves as both an invitation and a guarantee. It is an invitation that everyone who desires may come to God and find eternal salvation through His Son, Jesus Christ. "Look to Me, and be saved, all you ends of the earth! For I am God, and there is no other" (Isaiah 45:22). Jesus said, "Come to Me, all you who labor and are heavy laden, and I will give you rest" (Matthew 11:28). The Bible concludes with a universal invitation, "Let him who thirsts come. Whoever desires, let him take the water of life freely" (Revelation 22:17).

The Invitation

This universal invitation is seen throughout God's Word. Immediately after man rebelled against God in the Garden, God extended His hand of reconciliation. While Adam and Even were hiding in shame, "they heard the voice of the Lord God walking in the garden in the cool of the day" (Genesis 3:8, KJV). The Bible tells us, "Then the Lord God called to Adam and said to him, 'Where are you?'" (Genesis 3:9). God reached out to Adam and Eve. He sought them; they did not seek Him. Implicit within His question was an invitation to come to Him. Only He could save them from their own predicament. Moments later, God would begin to explain His plan for the redemption of humankind when He confronted the serpent, Satan.

God said to Satan, "And I will put enmity between you and the woman, and between your seed and her Seed; He shall bruise your head, and you shall bruise His heel" (Genesis 3:15). Notice that the word "Seed" is capitalized here. Although some English translations of the Bible do not capitalize it in this verse, all of them should because it refers to Jesus Christ. In this simple statement, God introduces His plan to redeem humankind from sin through the ultimate Seed of the woman, Jesus Christ. God foretold that although Satan would harm Jesus at the cross ("bruise his heel"), Jesus would deliver the fatal blow to Satan by His resurrection from the dead. Jesus defeated death, hell, and the grave when He "bruised Satan's head" on Resurrection Sunday.

The word "Seed" in Hebrew is significant for another reason. The Hebrew word translated as "seed" is *zera*. It is fairly common in the Hebrew Old Testament, used 229 times. Sometimes it is translated *descendants* or *offspring*, but it always refers to the seed of a male, not a female. Hence, this passage has puzzled Hebrew scholars, particularly secular scholars, because it speaks of *her* Seed, referring to Eve's seed. Because *zera* refers to the seed of a male (namely, semen), and because women do not have semen, what does this verse mean? Those who believe, as I do, that the ultimate Author of the Bible is God, see in this passage another aspect of God's plan of redemption. God's use of "her Seed" is a veiled reference to the virgin birth of Christ.

The God-man, Jesus, would not be conceived by normal human means using the seed of a man. He would be conceived by the Holy Spirit (Matthew 1:20). Adam's sin is passed on to all humankind at conception. "Through one man sin entered the world, and death through sin, and thus *death spread to all men*" (Romans 5:12). David said, "Behold, I was brought forth in iniquity, and *in sin my mother conceived me*" (Psalm 51:5). Our very nature is corrupt and in need of redemption. One sinner can never pay the price for another sinner. Only a perfect human being can pay the sin debt for the world. That is why Jesus had to be born of a virgin.

> **Our very nature is corrupt and in need of redemption. One sinner can never pay the price for another sinner.**

Jesus does not have a sin nature. He is not a sinner, which is what qualifies Him to take the sin of the whole world on His shoulders and redeem mankind from sin's penalty. "In Him there is no sin" (1 John 3:5). "[God] made Him who knew no sin to be sin for us, that we might become the righteousness of God in Him" (2 Corinthians 5:21). We are redeemed by "the precious blood of Christ, as of a lamb without blemish and without spot" (1 Peter 1:19). Jesus Christ "committed no sin," Peter tells us (1 Peter 2:22).

Genesis 3:15, where God promises to provide redemption through the Seed of the woman, is considered the earliest reference to the Gospel in the Bible. Theologians call it the *protevangelium*—*proto*, meaning first; *evangelium*, meaning gospel. Thus, immediately after the Fall, God issued His invitation to be rescued from the penalty of sin, and this invitation goes forth just as loudly and clearly today. God's Word says, "Come now, and let us reason together. Though your sins are like scarlet, they shall be as white as snow; though they are red like crimson, they shall be as wool" (Isaiah 1:18). The Lord's message through Isaiah the prophet to Judah in the eighth century BC extends to all people of all times. "Incline your ear, and come to Me. Hear, and your soul shall live" (Isaiah 55:3).

Jesus told the Samaritan woman that "the Father is seeking" people to worship Him—that is, to come to Him through His Son, Jesus Christ (John 4:23). "For God did not send His Son into the world to condemn the world, but that the world through Him might be saved" (John 3:17). Jesus said, "And I, if I am lifted up from the earth, will draw all peoples to Myself" (John 12:32). Every person who hears the good news about Christ, and believes in Him alone for eternal salvation, receives the free gift of eternal life. "Faith comes by hearing, and hearing by the Word of God" (Romans 10:17).

The Holy Spirit is always at work convicting the world "of sin, and of righteousness, and of judgment" (John 16:8). Jesus said that one of the reasons for the convicting work of the Holy Spirit is because people "do not believe in Me" (John 16:9). He said, "Most assuredly, I say to you, he who hears My word and believes in Him who sent Me has everlasting life, and shall not come into judgment, but has passed from death into life" (John 5:24). He could not have been clearer when He said, "Most assuredly, I say to you, he

> **The Holy Spirit is always at work convicting the world "of sin, and of righteousness, and of judgment."**

who believes in Me has everlasting life" (John 6:47). Just as God sought Adam and Even in the Garden after they sinned; just as Jesus came to "seek and to save that which is lost" (Luke 19:10), the Spirit of God continues to seek the lost today (John 16:8). Come one, come all!

The Guarantee

Like the English advertising posters of centuries gone by, the Gospel message contains a guarantee as well. Jesus said, "The one who comes to Me I will by no means cast out" (John 6:37). He made this statement in the context of one of the most well-known miracles He performed during His earthly ministry: the feeding of the five thousand. This miracle, like all of His miracles, served as a sign to show that He is the Son of God who alone can forgive sin and impart life. After He fed five thousand people with only five loaves of bread and two small fish, Jesus went away to be alone for a while.

The next day, the crowds sought Him out and, perhaps prompted by the miraculous supper they had enjoyed the day before, brought up the experience of Moses and the Israelites in the wilderness when God had provided manna from heaven. They said, "What sign will You perform then, that we may see it and believe You? What work will You do? Our fathers ate the manna in the desert; as it is written, 'He gave them bread from heaven to eat'" (John 6:30–31). Jesus answered their question by using a metaphor about food.

Food was no doubt on everyone's mind because of the stunning events of the previous day. Jesus explained to them that food that provides physical nourishment is one thing; food that provides eternal life is much better. He said, "Most assuredly, I say to you, Moses did not give you the bread from heaven, but My Father gives you the true bread from heaven. For the bread of God is He who comes down from heaven and gives life to the world" (John 6:32–33). He was speaking of Himself, of course. As the Bread of Life, eternal life can only come through Him. He said, "I am the bread of life. He who comes to Me shall never hunger, and he who believes in Me shall never thirst" (John 6:35). Notice the invitation: "He who comes to Me…" And notice the guarantee: "…shall never hunger."

Even if you were the only one who needed salvation; even if you were the only one who showed up at the cross seeking redemption, Jesus still would have died for your sins. The Gospel is a "come one, come all" event. Not only are we guaranteed that no one will be turned away, the Gospel

The Gospel is a "come one, come all" event.

also guarantees that the gift of salvation can never be lost. To those who believe the Gospel, Jesus says, "I give them eternal life, and they shall never perish; neither shall anyone snatch them out of My hand" (John 10:28). According to the Bible, if you believe in Jesus Christ as the only One who can save you, you can "know that you have eternal life" (1 John 5:13).

Eternal life is not something you get when you die; it is something you get immediately when you believe the Gospel. Notice the present-tense verb in Jesus' statement, "Most assuredly, I

Eternal life is a present possession, not a future possibility.

say to you, he who believes in Me *has* everlasting life" (John 6:47). Eternal life is a present possession, not a future possibility. Jesus did not promise to give believers the *prospect* of eternal life or the *potential* for eternal life. He promised to give *eternal life* to all who believe. If eternal life could be lost, it has the wrong name. Eternal life, by definition, can never be lost or else it was never *eternal* to begin with.

The moment a person believes the Gospel, he is "sealed with the Holy Spirit of promise, who is the guarantee of our inheritance until the redemption of the purchased possession, to the praise of His glory" (Ephesians 1:13–14). The Bible says,

> Who shall separate us from the love of Christ? Shall trib-ulation, or distress, or persecution, or famine, or naked-ness, or peril, or sword? As it is written: "For Your sake we are killed all day long; We are accounted as sheep for the slaughter." Yet in all these things we are more than conquerors through Him who loved us. For I am persuaded that neither death nor life, nor angels nor principalities nor powers, nor things present nor things to come, nor height nor depth, nor any other created thing, shall be able to separate us from the love of God which is in Christ Jesus our Lord. (Romans 8:35–39)

Those who place their faith in Jesus Christ as the only One who can save them from the penalty of sin are "adopted as sons" (Galatians 4:5) and become "children of God" (John 1:12). To say that someone who has believed the Gospel could end up in hell would be to say that God would cast out a member of His own family—but Jesus promised, "The one who comes to Me I will by no means cast out" (John 6:37).

The Wrong Response

There are many reasons that a person may refuse God's free offer to have his sins forgiven and avoid the penalty of hell. Ultimately they all come down to unbelief. Jesus said, "He who believes in Him is not condemned; but he who does not believe is condemned already, because he has not believed in the name of the only begotten Son of God" (John 3:18). He said, "If you do not believe that I am He, you will die in your sins" (John 8:24). Unbelief is an eternally fatal explosion that can be caused by many types of bombs, however. What causes someone to respond to God's free offer of eternal life with unbelief? In the previous chapters we have looked at several reasons for this.

Some people refuse to believe the Gospel because, like the Athenian philosophers, they think they are intelligent enough to solve their sin problem on their own. Sadly, one day they will find out they were too smart for their own good. Sin is no respecter of persons; it does not care how smart you are. Only Jesus can forgive sin. Others refuse to believe because they do not even acknowledge their sin problem to begin with. They have adopted an "I'm OK You're OK" perspective, and they think they are fine the way they are. If you do not realize you are a sinner, you have no need of a Savior; and if you do not think you need a Savior, you will reject God's invitation to be saved.

For some people, the explosion of unbelief is caused by the bomb of pluralism. They have mistakenly accepted the "tomayto tomahto" approach to salvation that says anything goes; there is more than one way to be saved, they think. This approach makes Jesus a liar when He said, "I am the way, the truth, and the life. No one comes to the Father except through Me"

(John 14:6). One day, people who have adopted this false understanding about salvation will realize that Jesus was correct when He said, "Enter by the narrow gate; for wide is the gate and broad is the way that leads to destruction, and there are many who go in by it" (Matthew 7:13). Only those who enter through the "narrow gate" of faith in Him will be saved (Matthew 7:14).

Still others will end up in hell because they mistakenly think they can negotiate their way into heaven. Eternal life, they wrongly conclude, is gained by making a deal with God. Unfortunately for them, salvation is not a bilateral agreement; it is a unilateral gift. Nothing we can offer God at the negotiating table can counteract the penalty of sin. We must receive salvation as a free gift by faith.

> **Nothing we can offer God at the negotiating table can counteract the penalty of sin.**

Another bomb that leads to unbelief for many people is pride. The narcissism epidemic that has overtaken our culture makes it hard for people to humble themselves and accept help. "I've got this!" they think. Those who stiffen their necks, however, and refuse to accept God's free offer of salvation, will end up in hell someday.

There are others who decline God's invitation because they are deeply wounded and hurt. Their hearts are broken because of some personal tragedy and they blame God for it. They feel He cannot be trusted. Because their hearts are blinded by pain, they will not come to the only One who can heal their hurts and forgive their sin. For others, a failure to believe the Gospel comes down to the simple fact that they have never heard the Gospel. Those who need to be rescued from the penalty of sin must hear and believe the Good News that Jesus died and rose again to pay their personal penalty for sin. If you never hear the Gospel, you cannot believe the Gospel; and if you do not believe the Gospel, you will go to hell when you die.

Some people end up in hell not because they have never heard about Jesus, but because they have heard and believed a false gospel. They may have been told about Jesus' death and resurrection; they may understand sin and their need for redemption; but they have been told they can get salvation by "giving their life to Jesus" or "inviting Him into their heart," or "turning their life over to Christ," or "making a U-turn and changing their behavior," or some other unbiblical means. Sadly, none of these things can replace the one and only condition for receiving eternal life: *faith alone in Christ alone*. Not all that glitters is gold. Do not believe everything you hear. Those who believe a false gospel will end up in hell someday.

The problem of suffering in the world presents another challenge for some people when it comes believing the Gospel. There are those who reject God's free invitation to eternal life because they cannot comprehend why so many bad things happen to so many good people. What they have failed to recognize,

> **God is the solution to all of man's suffering, not the cause of it.**

however, is that suffering is not God's fault. He created a perfect world and humankind messed it up by sin. God is the solution to all of man's suffering, not the cause of it. One day He will "wipe away every tear from their eyes; there shall be no more death, nor sorrow, nor crying. There shall be no more pain, for the former things have passed away" (Revelation 21:4). Until then, we must trust Him even when life does not make sense.

Finally, there are many people who are simply too busy to respond to God's invitation. The distractions of life keep them from focusing on what matters most. They have prioritized other tasks and activities ahead of their eternal soul. Yet, putting off a decision about whether or not to believe the Gospel is risky. We are not promised tomorrow; today is the day of salvation. Do not let busyness blind you to the Gospel. The stakes are too high.

The Right Response

Although there are many reasons a person may reject the Gospel and end up in hell, we must never forget that there is *one reason no one ever has to go to hell.*

> **We are not promised tomorrow; today is the day of salvation.**

Jesus Christ has made it possible for anyone and everyone to receive forgiveness and eternal life as a free gift. "Come one, come all," God says. Salvation is freely offered, and it must be freely received. God will not force anyone to believe. You can go to hell, if you really want to; but God loves you so much that He sent His only Son to die in your place, pay your penalty, and rescue you from hell.

The invitation to eternal life is received in only one way: by faith. Just as a physical gift requires a means of receiving it—typically by reaching out your hands and taking hold of the gift—likewise, the gift of salvation is received through a particular means. Because salvation is not a physical gift that can be grasped with our hands, we must receive it through some other method. That method, according to

> **You can go to hell, if you really want to; but God loves you so much that He sent His only Son to die in your place, pay your penalty, and rescue you from hell.**

God's Word, is faith. More than 160 times the Bible conditions eternal life upon faith and faith alone. When your hands meet a gift and you take hold of it, the gift becomes yours. Similarly, when your faith meets the Gospel, you take possession of eternal life in that very moment. You are born again.

People can and do believe many things in life. However, there is only one thing that, when believed, rescues you from the penalty of sin and provides eternal life: *faith alone in Christ alone.* The Gospel message has been proclaimed far and wide. The invitation has been sent. It is up to you to respond.

> **Come to the table He's prepared for you**
> **The bread of forgiveness, the wine of release**
> **Come to the table and sit down beside Him**
> **The Savior wants you to join in the feast.**
>
> **Come to the table and see in His eyes**
> **The love that the Father has spoken**
> **And know you are welcome, whatever your crime**
> **For every commandment you've broken.**
>
> **For He's come to love you and not to condemn**
> **And He offers a pardon of peace**
> **If you'll come to the table, you'll feel in your heart**
> **The greatest forgiveness, the greatest release.**
>
> **Michael Card**

God's offer of eternal salvation is a "come one, come all" invitation. Will you come to Him today? Will you trust in Jesus Christ, the Son of God, to forgive your sin and give you the free gift of eternal life? Jesus said, "Most assuredly, I say to you, he who believes in Me has everlasting life" (John 6:47).

For Further Discussion

1. What is God's invitation in the Gospel message?
2. What is God's guarantee in the Gospel message?
3. Who is God's invitation to eternal life directed to?

4. Why do some people reject God's invitation to eternal life? What are some of the reasons people do not believe the Gospel?

5. Have you personally trusted in Jesus Christ and Him alone for the free gift of eternal life?

Afterword

As I mentioned in the preface, this book is written for both believers and unbelievers alike. To those who have already believed the Gospel and are born-again Christians, I hope this book provides some insight into human nature, and into the reasons so many people do not believe the Gospel. In this way, perhaps it will help you as you share the good news with those who desperately need to hear it. The ten reasons listed in this book are by no means comprehensive. There is no limit to Satan's deception, and there is no limit to the things that might blind someone's heart to the Gospel. Yet, in more than thirty years of formal Gospel ministry, I have identified these ten as some of the most common reasons that people are unwilling to place their faith in Jesus Christ, God's Son and our Savior.

For those of you who have not yet believed the Gospel, I pray, now that you have made it to the end of this book, that perhaps you will realize just how plain and simple God's good news really is. I hope this book has challenged you to think differently about God. God loves you. He sent His Son to die in your place. Jesus rose from the dead, having paid your personal penalty for sin. He offers to you the free gift of forgiveness and eternal life if you will simply trust Him, and Him alone, for it. Is there anything still keeping you from trusting Him today?

If I can ever be of assistance, or if you just need someone to talk to, please contact me at info@notbyworks.org.

J. B. Hixson

Bibliography

The Holy Bible: Authorized King James Version (KJV). 1998. Nashville, TN: Holman Bible Publishers.

The Holy Bible: English Standard Version (ESV). 2001. Wheaton, IL: Crossway Bibles.

The Holy Bible: New American Standard (NAS). 2002. Anaheim, CA: Foundation Publications.

The Holy Bible: New International Version, 1984 (NIV). 1984. Grand Rapids, MI: Zondervan.

The Holy Bible: New King James Version (KJV). 2015. Nashville, TN: Thomas Nelson.

The Holy Bible: New Living Translation (NLT). 2015. Carol Stream, IL: Tyndale House.

Ali, Muhammad. n.d. "Muhammad Ali Quotes." Goodreads. https://www.goodreads.com/author/quotes/46261.Muhammad_Ali.

Altman, Daniel. 2011. *Newsweek*, July 17. https://www.newsweek.com/narcissism-rise-america-68509.

Anderson, Kerby. 1992. "Time and Busyness." Probe Ministries. http://leaderu.com/orgs/probe/docs/time.html.

Ariens, Chris. 2013. "Scott Pelley: 'We're Getting the Big Stories Wrong, Over and Over Again.'" TV Newser, May

10. https://www.adweek.com/tvnewser/scott-pelley-were-getting-the-big-stories-wrong-over-and-over-again/179884.

Arndt, William, Frederick W. Danker, Walter Bauer, and F. Wilbur Gingrich. 2000. *A Greek-English Lexicon of the New Testament and Other Early Christian Literature*, 3rd ed. Chicago, IL: University of Chicago Press.

Barclay, William. 1976. *The Acts of the Apostles*. Philadelphia, PA: The Westminster John Knox Press.

Becker, Margaret. 1989. "Just Come In." Genius. 1989. https://genius.com/Margaret-becker-just-come-in-lyrics.

Berne, Eric. 1964. *Games People Play*. New York: Grove Press.

Boice, James Montgomery. 1999. *The Glory of God's Grace: The Meaning of God's Grace—and How It Can Change Your Life*. Grand Rapids, MI: Kregel Publications.

Bonaparte, Napoleon. n.d. "What Is History, but a Fable Agreed upon." BrainyQuote. https://www.brainyquote.com/quotes/napoleon_bonaparte_105736. (Quote widely attributed to Napoleon, but actual source unknown. Ralph Waldo Emerson used this line and attributed it to Napoleon.)

Brown, Francis, S. R. Driver, Charles A. Briggs, Edward Robinson, James Strong, and Wilhelm Gesenius. 2015. *The Brown, Driver, Briggs Hebrew and English Lexicon: With an Appendix Containing the Biblical Aramaic: Coded with the Numbering System from Strong's Exhaustive Concordance of the Bible*. Peabody, MA: Hendrickson Publishers.

Butler, Heather A. 2017. "Why Do Smart People Do Foolish Things?" *Scientific American*, October 3, 2017. https://www.scientificamerican.com/article/why-do-smart-people-do-foolish-things.

Campbell, Donald K. 1985. "Joshua." *In Bible Knowledge Commentary: An Exposition of the Scriptures*, ed. John F. Walvoord and Roy B. Zuck, 325–71. Wheaton, IL: Victor Books.

Card, Michael. 1985. "Scandalon." Genius. https://genius.com/Michael-card-scandalon-lyrics.

Card, Michael. 1991. "Come to the Table." Song Lyrics. http://www.songlyrics.com/card-michael/come-to-the-table-lyrics.

Carmichael, Ralph. 1958. "The Savior Is Waiting." Song Lyrics. http://www.songlyrics.com/heritage-singers/the-savior-is-waiting-lyrics.

Carson, D. A. 2011. *The Gagging of God: Christianity Confronts Pluralism*. Grand Rapids, MI: Zondervan.

Casserly, Meghan. 2012. "If Time Is Money, Millennials Are Broke—And They Couldn't Be Happier." *Forbes Magazine*, September 5. https://www.forbes.com/sites/meghancasserly/2012/09/05/if-time-is-money-millennials-are-broke-busy-obsessed.

Chafer, Lewis Sperry. 1926. *Major Bible Themes*. Philadelphia, PA: Sunday School Times.

Chafer, Lewis Sperry. 1930. *True Evangelism*. London: Marshall & Co.

Chafer, Lewis Sperry. 1947. *Salvation*. Chicago, IL: Moody Press.

Chafer, Lewis Sperry. 1947. *Chafer Systematic Theology*. Dallas, TX: Dallas Seminary Press.

Chafer, Lewis Sperry. 1947. *Grace*. Chicago, IL: Moody Press.

Chafer, Lewis Sperry. 1990. *Satan: His Motives and Methods*. Grand Rapids, MI: Kregel.

Churchill, Winston. n.d. "History Will Be Kind to Me, for I Intend to Write It." BrainyQuote. https://www.brainyquote. com/quotes/winston_churchill_161247. (Quote widely attributed to Churchill, but actual source unknown.)

Clarke, Harry D. 1924. "Into My Heart." Hymn Time. http:// www.hymntime.com/tch/htm/i/m/y/imyheart.htm.

Constable, Thomas L. 2004. *Tom Constable's Expository Notes on the Bible*. Galaxie Software.

Darwin, Charles. 1886. *The Principal Works of Charles Darwin: The Origin of Species; The Descent of Man*. New York: John B. Alden.

DeGroat, Chuck. 2020. *When Narcissism Comes to Church: Healing Your Community from Emotional and Spiritual Abuse*. Downers Grove, IL: InterVarsity Press.

Dever, Mark, and Paul Alexander. 2005. *The Deliberate Church: Building Your Ministry on the Gospel*. Wheaton, IL: Crossway Books.

Einstein, Albert. n.d. "Condemnation without Investigation ...." AZ Quotes. https://www.azquotes.com/quote/598772. (Quote widely attributed to Einstein, but actual source unknown.)

Einstein, Albert. n.d. "The Only Thing More Dangerous ...." AZ Quotes. https://www.azquotes.com/quote/613503. (Quote widely attributed to Einstein, but actual source unknown.)

Enns, Paul P. 2014. *The Moody Handbook of Theology: Revised and Expanded*. Chicago, IL: Moody Publishers.

Ettensohn, Mark, and Jane Simon. 2016. *Unmasking Narcissism: A Guide to Understanding the Narcissist in Your Life.* Berkeley, CA: Althea Press.

Feinberg, Mortimer R., and John J. Tarrant, *Why Smart People Do Dumb Things* (New York: Fireside/Simon & Schuster, 1995).

Fernando, Ajith. 2000. "The Urgency of the Gospel." *In Telling the Truth: Evangelizing Postmoderns*, 371–83. Grand Rapids, MI: Zondervan.

Francis of Assisi. n.d. "Preach the Gospel at All Times …." AZ Quotes. https://www.azquotes.com/author/616-Francis_of_Assisi. (Quote widely attributed to St. Francis of Assisi, but actual source/speaker unknown.)

"Friends: Major Shampoo Explosion." YouTube (television episode). Accessed April 14, 2020. https://www.youtube.com/watch?v=4ekMeEE1FVU.

Gibb, Barry, and Robin Gibb. 1971. "How Can You Mend a Broken Heart?" Lyricsfreak. 1971. https://www.lyricsfreak.com/b/bee gees/how can you mend a broken heart_20015649.html.

Goethe, Johann Wolfgang von. 1809/1913. *Die Wahlverwandtschaften*. Berlin: Morawe & Scheffelt.

Guinness, Os. 1993. "I Believe in Doubt: Using Doubt to Strengthen Faith." In *Doubt and Assurance*, ed. R. C. Sproul, 31–35. Grand Rapids, MI: Baker.

Guinness, Os. 1996. *God in the Dark: The Assurance of Faith beyond a Shadow of Doubt*. Wheaton, IL: Crossway Books.

Hall, Elvina. 1865. "Jesus Paid It All." Hymnary. 1865. https://hymnary.org/text/i_hear_the_savior_say_thy_strength_indee.

Harris, Thomas A. 1969. *I'm OK — You're OK*. London: Pan.

Hendricks, Howard. 1990, September. "Hermeneutics Class Lecture." Dallas Theological Seminary.

Hewitt, Eliza Edmunds. 1891. "My Faith Has Found a Resting Place." https://library.timelesstruths.org/music/My_Faith_Has_Found_a_Resting_Place.

Hightower, Jim. n.d. "The Opposite of Courage …." BrainyQuote. https://www.brainyquote.com/quotes/jim_hightower_368748.

Hixson, J. B. 2011. *The Gospel Unplugged: Good News Plain and Simple*. Brenham, TX: Lucid Books.

Hixson, J. B. 2012. *The Great Last Days Deception: Exposing Satan's New World Order Agenda*. Brenham, TX: Lucid Books.

Hixson, J. B. 2013. *Getting the Gospel Wrong: The Evangelical Crisis No One Is Talking About*. Duluth, MN: Grace Gospel Press.

Hixson, J. B., and Mark Fontecchio. 2013. *What Lies Ahead: A Biblical Overview of the End Times*. Brenham, TX: Lucid Books.

Hixson, J. B., Rick B. Whitmire, and Roy B. Zuck, eds. 2012. *Freely by His Grace: Classical Free Grace Theology*. Duluth, MN: Grace Gospel Press.

Huxley, Aldous. n.d. "Facts Do Not Cease to Exist …." Goodreads. https://www.goodreads.com/quotes/1502-facts-do-not-cease-to-exist-because-they-are-ignored. (Quote widely attributed to Huxley, but actual source unknown.)

Jones, Ernest. 1981. *The Life and Work of Sigmund Freud. Vol. 1.* New York: Basic Books.

Kennedy, D. James. 1970. *Evangelism Explosion.* Wheaton, IL: Tyndale House.

Kluger, Jeffrey. 2015. T*he Narcissist Next Door: Understanding the Monster in Your Family, in Your Office, in Your Bed, in Your World.* New York: Riverhead.

Köhler, Ludwig, and Walter Baumgartner. 1999. *The Hebrew and Aramaic Lexicon of the Old Testament.* Leiden: Brill.

Kreider, Tim. 2012. "The 'Busy' Trap." *New York Times*, June 30, 2012. https://opinionator.blogs.nytimes.com/2012/06/30/the-busy-trap.

Lee, Johnny. 1980. "Looking for Love in All the Wrong Places." Metro Lyrics. https://www.metrolyrics.com/looking-for-love-lyrics-johnny-lee.html.

Lewis, C. S. 1996. *Mere Christianity.* New York: Simon & Schuster.

Lightner, Robert P. 1996. *Sin, the Savior, and Salvation: The Theology of Everlasting Life.* Grand Rapids, MI: Kregel Publications.

Litfin, Duane. 2012. "Works and Words: Why You Can't Preach the Gospel with Deeds." *Christianity Today*, May 30. https://www.christianitytoday.com/ct/2012/may/litfin-gospel-deeds.html.

Louw, Johannes P., and Eugene Albert Nida. 1996. *Greek-English Lexicon of the New Testament Based on Semantic Domains.* New York: United Bible Societies.

MacArthur, John F. 1990. "Faith According to the Apostle James." *Journal of the Evangelical Theological Society* 33 (March 1990): 13–34.

MacArthur, John. 1993. *Faith Works: The Gospel According to the Apostles.* Dallas, TX: Word.

MacArthur, John. 2003. *Hard to Believe: The High Cost and Infinite Value of Following Jesus.* Nashville, TN: Thomas Nelson Publishers.

MacArthur, John. 2008. *The Gospel According to Jesus: What Is Authentic Faith?* Grand Rapids, MI: Zondervan.

Malkin, Craig. 2015. *Rethinking Narcissism: The Secret to Recognizing and Coping with Narcissists.* New York: Harper Perennial.

Morris, Leila Naylor. 1898. "Let Jesus Come Into Your Heart." Hymnary. 1898. https://hymnary.org/text/if_you_are_tired_of_the_load_of_your_sin.

Morrow, Lance. 2001. "Evil." *Time*, June 24. http://content.time.com/time/magazine/article/0,9171,157219,00.html.

National Center for Health Statistics. 2020. *NCHS Fact Sheet.* https://www.cdc.gov/nchs/data/factsheets/factsheet_NVSS.pdf.

Orwell, George. n.d. "Who Controls the Past ...." Goodreads. https://www.goodreads.com/quotes/6145-who-controls-the-past-controls-the-future-who-controls-the. (Quote widely attributed to Orwell, but actual source unknown.)

Osteen, Joel. 2004. *Your Best Life Now: 7 Steps to Living Your Full Potential.* New York: FaithWords.

Osteen, Joel. 2005, June 20. *Larry King Live* appearance.

Osteen, Joel. 2006, December 22. *Larry King Live* appearance.

Packer, J. I. 1993. *Concise Theology: A Guide to Historic Christian Beliefs*. Wheaton, IL: Tyndale House.

Paley, William. 1879. "There Is a Principle Which Is a Bar … ." Goodreads. https://www.goodreads.com/quotes/18629-there-is-a-principle-which-is-a-bar-against-all.

Peale, Norman Vincent. 1952. *The Power of Positive Thinking*. Englewood Cliffs, NJ: Prentice-Hall.

Peterson, Eugene H. T*he Holy Bible: The Message*. 2013. Carol Stream, IL: NavPress.

Piper, John. 2006. *What Jesus Demands from the World*. Wheaton, IL: Crossway.Ratner, Paul. 2016. "Your Lifetime by the Numbers." Big Think, May 20. https://bigthink.com/paul-ratner/how-many-days-of-your-life-do-you-have-sex-your-lifetime-by-the-numbers.

Reji, Rhea. 2019. "Being Arrogant Is Good." *Trending US*, December 17. https://www.trendingus.com/reasons-why-good-being-arrogant.

Robson, David. 2019. *The Intelligence Trap: Why Smart People Make Dumb Mistakes*. New York: W. W. Norton.

Rogers, Adrian. 2018. "Worry Is a Mild Form of Atheism." *Crosswalk*. January 14. https://www.crosswalk.com/devotionals/loveworthfinding/love-worth-finding-january-14-2018.html.

Rokser, Dennis. 2014. *Don't Ask Jesus Into Your Heart: A Biblical Answer to the Question: "What Must I Do to Be Saved?"* Duluth, MN: Grace Gospel Press.

Roosevelt, Franklin D. "You Are Just an Extra in Everybody Else's Play." BrainyQuote. https://www.brainyquote.com/quotes/franklin_d_roosevelt_162884. (Quote widely attributed to Roosevelt, but actual source unknown.)

Ryrie, Charles Caldwell. 1997. *So Great Salvation: What It Means to Believe in Jesus Christ.* Chicago, IL: Moody Press.

Ryrie, Charles Caldwell. 1999. *Basic Theology: A Popular Systemic Guide to Understanding Biblical Truth.* Chicago, IL: Moody Press.

Ryrie, Charles Caldwell. 2007. *Dispensationalism.* Chicago, IL: Moody Publishers.

Santayana, George. n.d. "Those Who Cannot Remember the Past …." Goodreads. https://www.goodreads.com/quotes/tag/doomed-to-repeat-it. (Quote widely attributed to Santayana, but actual source unknown.)

Schulte, Brigid. 2014. *Overwhelmed: Work, Love, and Play When No One Has the Time.* New York: Sarah Crichton Books.

Shahbazian, Steve. n.d. "Steve Shahbazian Quotes." Good Reads. https://www.goodreads.com/author/quotes/19374107. Steve_Shahbazian. (See also https://steveshahbazian.com)

Shakespeare, William. 2001. *Henry V*, ed. Roma Gill. Oxford: Oxford University Press.

Shakespeare, William. 2008. *Macbeth*, ed. Anne Collins. Harlow, England: Pearson Education.

Shockley, Paul R. 1998. "Postmodernism as a Basis for Society?" In *The God of the Bible and Other Gods: Is the Christian God Unique among World Religions?*, ed. Robert P. Lightner, 197–209. Grand Rapids, MI: Kregel.

Shockley, Paul R. 2000. "The Postmodern Theory of Probability on Evangelical Hermeneutics." *Conservative Theological Society Journal* 4 (April 2000): 65–82.

Smith, Colin S. 2000. "The Ambassador's Job Description." In *Telling the Truth: Evangelizing Postmoderns*, ed. D. A. Carson, 175–91. Grand Rapids, MI: Zondervan.

Sproul, R. C. 1992. *Before the Face of God: A Daily Guide for Living from the Book of Romans*. Orlando, FL: Ligonier Ministries.

Sproul, R. C. 1993. "The Anatomy of Doubt." In *Doubt and Assurance*, ed. R. C. Sproul, 15–19. Grand Rapids, MI: Baker.

Sproul, R. C. 1994. *Before the Face of God: A Daily Guide for Living from Ephesians, Hebrews, and James*. Orlando, FL: Ligonier Ministries.

Sproul, R. C. 1994. *Before the Face of God: A Daily Guide for Living from the Old Testament*. Orlando, FL: Ligonier Ministries.

Sproul, R. C. 1994. *Chosen by God*. Wheaton, IL: Tyndale House.

Sproul, R. C. 1997. *Grace Unknown: The Heart of Reformed Theology*. Grand Rapids, MI: Baker Book House.

Sproul, R. C. 1998. *Essential Truths of the Christian Faith*. Wheaton, IL: Tyndale House.

Sproul, R. C. 1999. *Getting the Gospel Right: The Tie that Binds Evangelicals Together*. Grand Rapids, MI: Baker Book House.

Sproul, R. C. 2000. *Faith Alone: The Evangelical Doctrine of Justification*. Grand Rapids, MI: Baker Books.

Stein, Joel. 2013. "Millennials: The Me, Me, Me Generation." *Time*, May 20. https://time.com/247/millennials-the-me-me-me-generation.

Stockton, John. 1874. "Only Trust Him." Hymnary. 1874. https://hymnary.org/text/come_every_soul_by_sin_oppressed_theres.

Stott, John R. W. 1971. *Basic Christianity* (2d ed.). London: Inter-Varsity Press.

Swindoll, Charles R. 1990. *The Grace Awakening*. Dallas, TX: Word.

Swindoll, Charles R. 2003. *Simple Faith*. Nashville, TN: Word.

Taylor, Jim. 2011. "Narcissism: On the Rise in America?" *Huffpost*, May 28. https://www.huffpost.com/entry/narcissism-america_b_861887.

Thomas, Robert L. 1998. *New American Standard Hebrew-Aramaic and Greek Dictionaries: Updated Edition*. Anaheim, CA: Lockman Foundation.

Tolstoy, Leo. n.d. "History Would Be a Wonderful Thing …." Goodreads. https://www.goodreads.com/quotes/87536-history-would-be-a-wonderful-thing-if-it-were. (Quote widely attributed to Tolstoy, but actual source unknown.)

Toplady, Augustus. 1763. "Rock of Ages." Wikipedia. 1763. https://en.wikipedia.org/wiki/Rock_of_Ages_(Christian_hymn).

Trump, Donald J. "Trump Tweets." Trump Twitter Archive. http://trumptwitterarchive.com.

Trump, Donald J., and Tony Schwartz. 1987. *Trump: The Art of the Deal*. New York: Random House.

Trump, Donald, and Meredith McIver. 2008. *Trump Never Give Up: How I Turned My Biggest Challenges into Success*. Hoboken, NJ: John Wiley & Sons.

Twain, Mark. n.d. "It Is Easier to Fool People ...." Goodreads. https://www.goodreads.com/quotes/584507-it-s-easier-to-fool-people-than-to-convince-them-that. (Quote widely attributed to Twain, but actual source unknown.)

Twain, Mark. n.d. "The Very Ink with Which History Is Written ...." BrainyQuote. https://www.brainyquote.com/quotes/mark_twain_105745. (Quote widely attributed to Twain, but actual source unknown.)

"US Life Expectancy Drops for Second Year in a Row." 2017. *CNN*, December 21. https://lite.cnn.com/en/article/h_0ed105c5c32f3537d7e304e4bcde0e18.

"Verizon Wireless 'Can You Hear Me Now?'" n.d. YouTube video. Accessed April 14, 2020. https://www.youtube.com/watch?v=Lo0xsZCRp4g.

Voltaire. n.d. "It Is Difficult to Free Fools ...." BrainyQuote. https://www.brainyquote.com/quotes/voltaire_136298. (Quote widely attributed to Voltaire, but actual source.)

Voltaire. n.d. "One Great Use of Words ...." BrainyQuote. https://www.brainyquote.com/quotes/voltaire_141036. (Quote widely attributed to Voltaire, but actual source.)

Voltaire. n.d. "Those Who Can Make You Believe Absurdities ...." BrainyQuote. https://www.brainyquote.com/quotes/voltaire_118641.

Waltke, Bruce. n.d. "Class Lecture on Psalm 90." Dallas Theological Seminary. Accessed from cassette tape; original date of recording unknown.

Walvoord, John F. 1991. *The Holy Spirit.* Grand Rapids, MI: Zondervan.

Walvoord, John F., and Roy B. Zuck. 1985. *Bible Knowledge Commentary: An Exposition of the Scriptures.* Wheaton, IL: Victor Books.

Warfield, Benjamin B., and John E. Meeter. 1980. *Selected Shorter Writings of Benjamin B. Warfield.* Phillipsburg, NJ: Presbyterian and Reformed Publishing.

Watterson, Bill. 2012. *The Complete Calvin and Hobbes.* Kansas City, MO: Andrew McMeel.

"Wendy's 'Where's the Beef?.'" n.d. YouTube video. Accessed April 14, 2020. https://www.youtube.com/watch?v=riH5EsGcmTw.

Williams, Zoe. 2016. "Me! Me! Me! Are We Living through a Narcissism Epidemic?" *The Guardian*, March 2, 2016. https://www.theguardian.com/lifeandstyle/2016/mar/02/narcissism-epidemic-self-obsession-attention-seeking-oversharing.

Wright, Susan. 2016. "Hey, Christians: Trump Says Winning the White House Will Get Him to Heaven." Red State. August 12, 2016. https://www.redstate.com/sweetie15/2016/08/12/hey-christians-trump-says-winning-white-house-will-get-heaven.

Zappa, Frank. n.d. "A Mind Is like a Parachute...." Goodreads. https://www.goodreads.com/quotes/33052-a-mind-is-like-a-parachute-it-doesn-t-work-if.

About the Author

J. B. Hixson serves as the founder and president of Not By Works Ministries. Since 1999, Not By Works has been committed to promoting the clear, accurate, and urgent Gospel message. According to the Bible, eternal life is found only through faith in Jesus Christ alone, who died and rose again for our sins. Not By Works seeks to advance the message of God's amazing grace through a nationwide conference-speaking ministry; through the publication and distribution of books, DVDs, CDs, and other biblical resources; and through a daily radio program. For more information about hosting a Not By Works conference in your area, please visit www.NotByWorks.org.

Additionally, Dr. Hixson is a pastor, professor, and national conference speaker. He earned his BA degree from Houston Baptist University; ThM degree from Dallas Theological Seminary; and PhD degree from Baptist Bible Seminary. Dr. Hixson has been involved in pastoral and academic ministry since 1987. He is the author or editor of several books, including *Getting the Gospel Wrong, The Gospel Unplugged, The Great Last Days Deception, What Lies Ahead, The NBW Book of Theological Charts, Diagrams, & Illustrations*, and *Freely by His Grace*. He also has written for or contributed to numerous theological journals, magazines, newspapers, blogs, and newsletters.

J. B. and his wife, Wendy, have six children and one grandchild.

Other Titles from Grace Acres Press

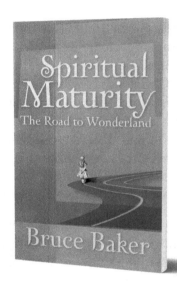

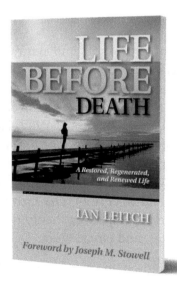

Other Titles from Grace Acres Press

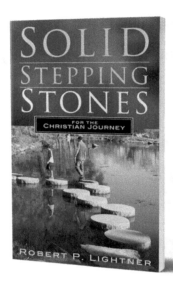

Available at GraceAcresPress.com
or wherever books are sold.

Printed in the USA
CPSIA information can be obtained
at www.ICGtesting.com
LVHW020809141123
763765LV00013B/112